Date Due

APR 2 5 1995		

909.5
Mar

Martell, Hazel.
The age of discovery

909.5
Mar

Martell, Hazel.
The age of discovery

THE ILLUSTRATED HISTORY OF THE WORLD

1
The Earliest Civilizations

2
Rome and the Ancient World

3
The Dark Ages

4
The Middle Ages

5
The Age of Discovery
(1 5 0 0 – 1 6 5 0)

6
Conflict and Change
(1 6 5 0 – 1 8 0 0)

7
The Nineteenth Century

8
The Modern World

The Age of Discovery

PREFACE

*T*he Illustrated History of the World is a unique series of eight volumes covering the entire scope of human history, from the days of the nomadic hunters up to the present. Each volume surveys significant events and personages, key political and economic developments, and the critical forces that inspired change, in both institutions and the everyday life of people around the globe.

The books are organized on a spread-by-spread basis, allowing ease of access and depth of coverage on a wide range of fascinating topics and time periods within any one volume. Each spread serves as a kind of mini-essay, in words and pictures, of its subject. The text—cogent, concise and lively—is supplemented by an impressive array of illustrations (original art, full-color photographs, maps, diagrams) and features (glossary, index, time charts, further reading listings). Taking into account the new emphasis on multicultural education, special care has been given to presenting a balanced portrait of world history: the volumes in the series explore all civilizations— whether it's the Mayans in Mexico, the Shoguns in Japan or the Sumerians in the Middle East.

The Age of Discovery

Hazel Mary Martell

Facts On File

Library of Congress Cataloging-in-Publication Data

Martell, Hazel.
The age of discovery/ Hazel Mary Martell.
p.   cm. — (Illustrated history of the world)
Includes bibliographical references and index.
Summary: Explores the history of the world from 1500 to 1650, an
active period which included the Renaissance in Europe, European
explorations among the ancient empires of Africa and South America,
and the decline of the Mogul Empire in India.
ISBN 0-8160-2789-7
1. History, Modern—16th century—Juvenile literature.
2. History, Modern—17th century—Juvenile literature.
[1. History, Modern—16th century. 2. History, Modern—17th
century.] I. Title. II. Series: Illustrated history of the world
(New York, N.Y.)
D228.M37 1993
909.5—dc20
92-18621
CIP
AC

ISBN 0 8160 2789 7

Facts On File books are available at special discounts when purchased
in bulk quantities for businesses, associations, institutions or sales
promotions. Please call our Special Sales Department in New York at
212/683-2244 (dial 800/322-8755 except in NY, AK or HI).

Designed by Hammond Hammond
Composition by Goodfellow and Egan Ltd, Cambridge
Printed and Bound by BPCC Hazell Books, Paulton and Aylesbury

10 9 8 7 6 5 4 3 2 1

This book is printed on acid-free paper.

First Published in Great Britain in 1991 by
Simon and Schuster Young Books

CONTENTS

The period from 1500 to 1650 was a period of great activity in all fields of human endeavor. It was a time when scholars were expanding the limits of their knowledge, rulers were trying to expand the limits of their territories, and even ordinary people were beginning to question traditional ideas and beliefs.

All of this was especially true in Europe, where the *Renaissance* in the fifteenth century had led to a revival of learning, as well as an interest in humanity and the natural world. This expansion of thought and knowledge led to conflicts over religion which lasted throughout the period. It also led to advances in science and technology. In spite of the constant threat of war and disease, art and literature flourished.

There was also a spirit of adventure which encouraged men at this time to set out and sail further than any Europeans had done since the age of the Vikings. They looked for new trading routes, especially to the spice-producing countries of the Far East. They also searched for treasure and for land to colonize as parts of Europe became overcrowded.

Beyond Europe, other parts of the world were undergoing great change too. The Ottoman Empire reached its peak at this time and was able to threaten Europe by land and by sea. In India, Babur founded the Mogul Dynasty in 1526 and his grandson Akbar ruled over a large empire. Russia started to expand as the *Tartars* were finally overthrown, while in Africa the Songhai Empire grew as its trade increased. In China the Ming Dynasty was firmly established and in Japan the Tokugawa shogunate brought peace to a troubled land.

By 1650, however, the European powers had started to dominate the world. Spain, Portugal, England, France and the Netherlands had set up trading posts and colonies throughout Africa, Asia and America. Within another 50 years, large areas of these continents would be parts of vast European empires.

Empire of Charles V

Lithuania

Swedish Empire after 1523

Denmark and Norway

Poland

SCANDINAVIA

SCOTLAND

RUSSIA

ENGLAND

LONDON •

• AMSTERDAM

LITHUANIA

NETHERLANDS

GERMAN
STATES

POLAND

PARIS •

FRANCE

AUSTRIA

VENICE •

SPAIN

MADRID •

ITALY

OTTOMAN

• CONSTANTINOPLE

EMPIRE

PART ONE

Conflicts in Europe

The years from 1500 to 1650 mark the change from the *Middle Ages* to the Europe we know today. The changes did not come suddenly in 1500, however. Some things had already started to alter before then, while others were much the same by 1650. For example, many people still died as a result of warfare, famine and disease, just as they had done in the Middle Ages. Many children died before their first birthday and few people lived to be 70.

Most people still lived and worked in the country, but by 1500 towns were growing in size. This was partly because the population had finally got back to the level it had reached before the *Black Death* struck in 1347–48, and had then started to increase. As a result, there was not enough land for everyone and so some people went to seek a living in towns.

EUROPEAN KINGDOMS Another change was the rise of powerful monarchs in Spain, France and England. These monarchs set up governments to rule over a whole country, instead of just a part of it. The boundaries of some kingdoms were different from today, however. For example, the kings and queens of England ruled over Wales and Ireland, as well as over Calais in France until

1558. Scotland had its own ruler, but the Netherlands was governed by the Spanish monarch, who also ruled Portugal from 1580 to 1640. Italy was divided into many small states and kingdoms. Because many of these were rich, the French and Spanish both tried to conquer them and make them part of their empires.

Germany was divided into small states and was part of the *Holy Roman Empire*, which included Austria, parts of northern Italy, Hungary and Czechoslovakia. It was usually ruled by the Habsburg family.

ART AND RELIGION The greatest change in this period was in people's outlook on life, as a result of the Renaissance, which had started in Italy in the fourteenth century. People became more interested in the world about them. Artists painted portraits and landscapes, as well as religious subjects. Sculptors carved life-like statues. Other people studied things scientifically, instead of just accepting what they were told.

As these new ideas spread, some people began to question the teachings of the Church. This led to serious conflict, which lasted throughout the period. By 1650 many people had died for their beliefs and many others had fled overseas to escape *persecution*.

Conflict Over Religion
THE REFORMATION

Desiderius Erasmus and Thomas More

Above. Sir Thomas More.

Right. Desiderius Erasmus.

Erasmus (1466–1536), one of the most influential scholars of the Renaissance period, was born in Rotterdam. He studied and taught all over Europe, including France, England, Italy and Switzerland.

In 1516 Erasmus made the first translation of the New Testament from Greek into Latin, which won him the support of many critics of the Roman Catholic Church.

Erasmus was opposed to the power of the priests and to the corruption within the Church. He gave some support to Martin Luther, but he remained a Roman Catholic priest all his life.

Sir Thomas More (1477–1535), an English lawyer and scholar, was one of Henry VIII's advisors. He became Chancellor in 1529, but resigned in protest in 1532 when the king declared himself head of the English Church. In 1535 he was beheaded for treason after false evidence was used against him.

His most famous work was a book called *Utopia*, which was about an ideal social and political system.

As new ideas about life and religion spread across Europe, some people began to want to reform the Catholic Church, because they thought it had grown too powerful and too greedy. They also thought it had moved away from its spiritual work and was more concerned with worldly matters, such as making money. For example, some popes gave important jobs within the Church to their friends and relations in exchange for expensive gifts. Others also made money by accepting payments for letting priests have more than one *parish*, or allowing bishops to have more than one *diocese*, even though this was against the rules of the Church. Money was also made by selling indulgences. These were certificates from the pope that people could buy from traveling salesmen, which they believed would release them from doing a *penance* for their sins.

MARTIN LUTHER One person who objected to the sale of indulgences was Martin Luther (1483–1546), a German priest who lived in Wittenberg. He believed that a person could only be saved through faith in God and not through good deeds on earth or by giving money to the Church. He felt so strongly about this that in 1517 he made out a list of things he thought were wrong with the Church and nailed it to the door of the church in Wittenberg.

Luther thought his list would lead to a debate among clergymen, which in turn would lead to reforms within the Church. Instead he found himself accused of heresy. When he refused to take back what he had said, the pope *excommunicated* him. By this time, however, his ideas were gaining support in northern Germany and Switzerland. At first his followers were called *Lutherans*. They became known as *Protestants* in 1529 when some of them went to the Diet (meeting) of Speyer and protested against restrictions on their teachings.

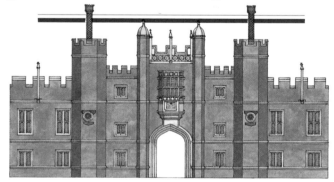

Hampton Court Palace

Hampton Court was built for Cardinal Wolsey, who entered Henry VIII's service in 1509 and became Bishop of Lincoln and then Archbishop of York.

He became a cardinal in 1515 and took advantage of this to make a huge fortune.

Wolsey gave Hampton Court to Henry VIII in the 1520s. He also tried to persuade the pope to allow Henry to divorce Catherine of Aragon. When he failed, he fell from power and died on his way to face trial in London.

Left. Around the time of the Reformation, there were many paintings, woodcut pictures and pamphlets which mocked some of the beliefs of the Roman Catholic Church. This is part of one of these paintings. It shows nuns, monks and priests trying to bite a loaf of bread as it swings from a rope in a tree. The artist was Hieronymus Bosch.

1 The Safavid Dynasty was founded in Persia (now Iran) by Shah Ismail in 1500. He established Shiism as the state religion and ruled until his death in 1524. Persia had a time of great prosperity between 1587 and 1629, then its fortunes started to decline. The Safavid Dynasty lasted until 1736.

2 In 1546 the people of the Songhai Empire destroyed the Mali Empire. In 1591 their own empire was destroyed by the Moroccans.

3 After the battle of Al Kasr al Kebir in 1578, the Moroccans destroyed the power of the Portuguese in the northwest of Africa.

4 In 1592–3 and 1597–8, the Japanese invaded Korea. On both occasions they were driven out by the Chinese.

ULRICH ZWINGLI One of Luther's earliest supporters was Ulrich Zwingli (1484–1531), a clergyman who started the Reformation in Switzerland in 1519 with his preaching in Zurich. He was more extreme in his views than Luther, and in 1524 he abolished the Catholic Mass (church service) in Zurich. This led to civil war in Switzerland, as some *cantons* wanted to remain Catholic instead of joining Zwingli's reformed cantons. The Catholics were eventually defeated, but not before Zwingli had been killed in battle.

JOHN CALVIN Another early leader of the Reformation was John Calvin (1509–1564), a Frenchman who had studied law and *theology*. In 1536 he went to Basle in Switzerland, where he published a book called *The Institutes of the Christian Religion*. In this book he set out his views on religion, which later influenced John Knox (1514–1572), the Scottish theologian who led the Reformation in Scotland in the mid-sixteenth century.

DISAGREEMENTS BETWEEN PROTESTANTS
Although both Luther and Calvin agreed that the Church needed to be reformed, they disagreed on other points. This led to a split among the Protestants, with some following Luther and others following Calvin.

Above. A portrait of Martin Luther, the German priest who started the Reformation.

Left. The French theologian, John Calvin.

11

THE SPREAD OF PROTESTANTISM

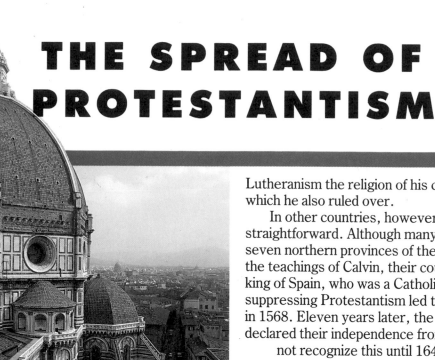

Catholic churches, like this cathedral in Florence, Italy, shown above, were very ornate. Inside, the walls were decorated with religious paintings. Protestant churches such as the one on the right were usually plain. There were no stained glass windows or statues.

Martin Luther's intentions to reform the Catholic Church led instead to the founding of Protestantism. Its followers rejected the leadership of the pope and many of the teachings of the Catholic Church. They built plain churches and concentrated on the teachings of the Bible and on preaching, rather than on the *holy sacraments*. They also stopped using Latin in their services and instead used the language of the country they were in so that everyone could understand what was being said.

NORTHERN EUROPE These new ideas soon became popular in northern Europe. By 1529, King Gustavus I (1523–1560) had made Lutheranism the religion of Sweden and Finland. In 1536 the king of Denmark made Lutheranism the religion of his country and of Norway, which he also ruled over.

In other countries, however, the changes were less straightforward. Although many of the people in the seven northern provinces of the Netherlands followed the teachings of Calvin, their country was ruled by the king of Spain, who was a Catholic. His attempts at suppressing Protestantism led to a revolt which started in 1568. Eleven years later, the seven provinces declared their independence from Spain, but Spain did not recognize this until 1648.

FRANCE Calvin's followers also had problems in France, where they were known as *Huguenots*. As their numbers grew, there was rivalry between their leaders and members of the influential Guise family, who were Roman Catholics. This rivalry led to a series of civil wars, known as the Wars of Religion, which started in 1562 and lasted until 1598, when Henry of Navarre became king of France and gave the Huguenots their religious freedom.

ENGLAND UNDER HENRY VIII In England the break with the Roman Catholic Church came as a result of a quarrel between Henry VIII (1509–1547) and Pope Clement VII (1523–1534). The king decided he wanted to divorce his wife, Catherine of Aragon, because she had not given him the son he wanted. He had to ask the pope for permission to do this and Clement refused to agree. Henry then decided to set up a new Church which would be under his control and which would allow him to divorce Catherine and marry Anne Boleyn. The new Church was not very much different from the Roman Catholic Church. Henry still thought of himself as a Catholic, but in the late 1530s he closed all the monasteries and convents and sold their land.

EDWARD VI After Henry was succeeded by his young son, Edward VI (1547–1553), the Church in England became much more Protestant. Statues and pictures were removed from churches and *wall-paintings* were covered with whitewash. Priests were allowed to marry and the heresy laws were abolished. In 1549 the first *Book of Common Prayer* was published.

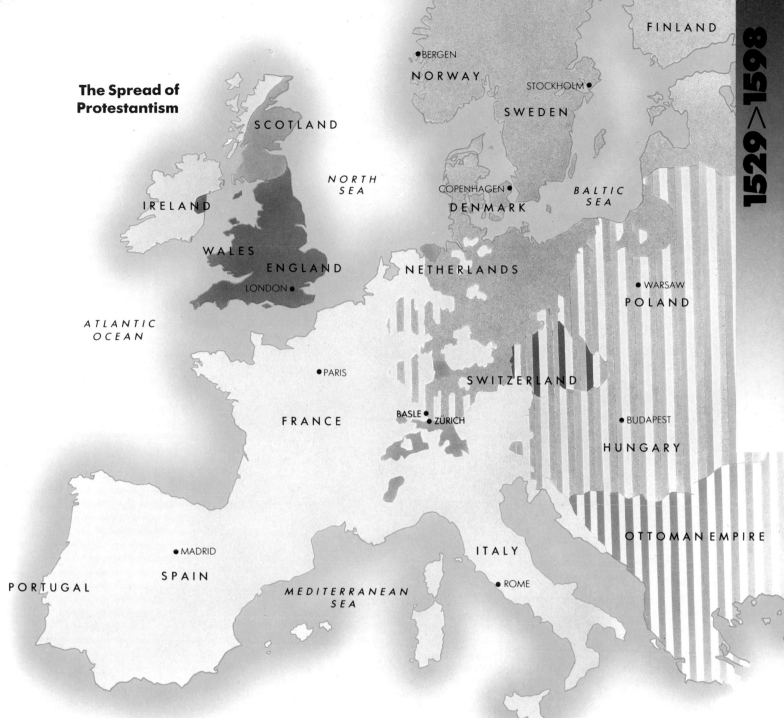

The Spread of Protestantism

FINLAND

BERGEN

NORWAY

STOCKHOLM

SWEDEN

SCOTLAND

NORTH SEA

COPENHAGEN

BALTIC SEA

IRELAND

DENMARK

WALES

ENGLAND

NETHERLANDS

WARSAW

LONDON

POLAND

ATLANTIC OCEAN

PARIS

SWITZERLAND

FRANCE

BASLE

ZÜRICH

BUDAPEST

HUNGARY

OTTOMAN EMPIRE

MADRID

ITALY

SPAIN

ROME

PORTUGAL

MEDITERRANEAN SEA

Right. The St. Bartholomew's Day Massacre took place in Paris in 1572. Catherine de' Medici, the mother of King Charles IX, encouraged the Catholic Guise family to shoot Coligny, a leading Protestant. Coligny was only wounded, but Catherine was afraid that the Huguenots would attack the palace in revenge. She persuaded her son to agree to the massacre of about 3000 Hugenots.

PARIS

Above. Europe was soon divided by religion. In general, countries to the north became Protestant, while those to the south remained Roman Catholic. The main problems arose in the countries where the rulers were Catholics but a large number of the people wanted to be Protestants. This was especially true in some north German states which belonged to the Holy Roman Empire. This led to the Thirty Years' War.

Roman Catholic

Lutheran

Calvinist

Hussite

Orthodox

Muslim

Anglican

THE COUNTER-REFORMATION

The Inquisition

Pope Gregory IX set up the Inquisition in 1231 to fight heresy. When it accused people of heresy, it used torture to make them confess. Those who confessed had to do a penance or pay a fine, while those who refused to confess were put in prison or executed by burning.

In 1478, the Inquisition was revived in Spain and used against Jews and Muslims. It became known as the Spanish Inquisition. After the Reformation, it was used against Protestants in Spain and later in the Netherlands.

Later, Pope Paul III set up the Roman Inquisition to try and stop heresy and the spread of Protestantism. One of its victims was the astronomer Galileo, who spent the last years of his life as a prisoner in his own house for saying that the earth moved round the sun.

Left. People who were condemned to death by the Inquisition were executed in public. Often several of them were burnt at once in the main square of a town. Special stands were constructed so that the crowds could see what was happening. The Spanish called these burnings an *Auto-da-Fé,* or Act of Faith.

Throughout the fifteenth century various people had tried to reform the Catholic Church, but they had not had much success. The Church had been too powerful and any signs of heresy or *dissent* had been stamped out. Once the Protestants rejected the pope's leadership, however, the Catholic Church realized that it had to look seriously at reforming itself. In 1522 Pope Adrian VI admitted that there was much wrong with the Church, but he died before he could make any changes.

Adrian VI was followed by Clement VII and, while he was pope, Rome was attacked and looted by troops of the Holy Roman Empire. Many people were killed and much damage was done to the city, its art treasures and its religious buildings. This attack was in 1527 and many Catholics saw it as a symbol of the collapse of the old Church. Nothing was done until 1534, however, when Paul III succeeded Clement VII as pope.

POPE PAUL III Realizing that the Church was in a crisis, Paul III (1534–1549) determined to try and solve its many problems. He started by encouraging the preaching

This reconstruction shows the Vatican in Rome. The popes have lived there since 1377, but it has been expanded many times since that date. It now has over 4000 rooms, including five museums and a library. The most famous room is probably the Sistine Chapel, which was built at the end of the fifteenth century and has a ceiling painted by Michelangelo. As well as being the residence of the pope, the Vatican is also the administrative centre for the Roman Catholic Church throughout the world. Since 1505 it has been guarded by its own private army called the Swiss Guard.

Left. Ignatius Loyola was born into a wealthy Spanish family in 1491. He started his career as a soldier, but after he was wounded in battle he became interested in religion. Loyola became a priest in 1534. He planned to preach to the Muslims, but Pope Paul III persuaded him to help the Catholic Church in its struggle against the Protestants.

Above. Mary I of England became known as "Bloody Mary" because of her persecution of Protestants. She was a devout woman who believed Protestantism was heresy.

and *missionary work* of the Capuchins, an order of friars which had been founded in Italy in 1525.

In 1540 he gave his approval to the Society of Jesus, or Jesuits, which Ignatius Loyola had founded in 1534 to spread the Catholic faith. As well as being missionaries, the Jesuits also set up schools and colleges. In countries where there were Protestants as well as Catholics, the Jesuits accepted children of both religions into their schools in the hope of converting the Protestants back to Catholicism.

THE COUNCIL OF TRENT Encouraged by the Holy Roman Emperor, Charles V (see p. 18), Paul III called the Council of Trent in 1545 to decide how the Catholic Church should be reformed. This Council met three times between 1545 and 1563 and made many important decisions. These included the setting up of colleges, or seminaries, so that priests could be better trained; a rule that bishops should live in their dioceses; and a rule that priests, nuns and monks should keep to their vows of poverty. The Council also agreed with the old beliefs of the Catholic Church, such as the importance of the holy sacraments, and *salvation* through good deeds on earth.

MARY I OF ENGLAND Charles V encouraged the Counter-Reformation still further in 1554 with the marriage of his son, Philip, the future king of Spain (see p. 19), to Mary I of England (1553–1558). Mary was the Catholic daughter of Henry VIII and Catherine of Aragon, who had made England into a Catholic country again when she became queen. She brought back the laws of heresy and soon began persecuting Protestants. Many fled abroad, but about 300 were burnt for their beliefs.

Philip left Mary when she had not given birth to a child after they had been married for 14 months, but he still was able to persuade her to join with Spain in a war against France in 1557. As a result England lost Calais. Mary's subjects never forgave her for this and few were sorry when she died.

15

THE GROWTH OF PURITANISM

When Elizabeth I (1558–1603) came to the throne after the death of her half-sister Mary, she made England into a Protestant country once more. Although she was only 25 years old when she became queen, Elizabeth already knew of the problems which could be caused by extreme religious views. She also knew that she had to reunite the country under her rule and get rid of the deep divisions caused by Mary's reign. She did this partly by giving the new Church of England features of both the Protestant and the Catholic Churches, saying that she wanted to create a "middle way." For example, there were still bishops, but now they were chosen by the queen and not by the pope. Churches were kept fairly plain, but priests still wore robes, called *vestments*, during the services.

THE FIRST PURITANS Most people accepted this new Church of England, but there were some who thought that it was not Protestant enough. Many of these people had lived in exile during Mary's reign and, influenced by the ideas of Calvin (see p. 11), did not approve of bishops. They also wanted to get rid of the priests' vestments and anything else that was left over from the old Catholic religion. They believed that this would purify the Church and, because of this belief, they became known as Puritans. As the number of Puritans grew, some became Members of Parliament and others became clergymen within the Church of England, thinking that holding these positions would help them to change the Church. In 1583, however, John Whitgift, the Archbishop of Canterbury, managed to make the Puritan clergymen leave the Church. In spite of this, the Puritan movement continued for the rest of Elizabeth's reign.

THE REIGN OF JAMES I Elizabeth I had no children and so when she died the throne of England passed to her nearest relation. This was her cousin, King James VI of Scotland, the son of Mary, Queen of Scots (1542–1567), who had been executed for *treason* by Elizabeth in 1587, 20 years after she had been *deposed* from the Scottish throne.

Mary's son became King James I of England (1603–1625). He persecuted Catholics and, although he met with the Puritans in 1604, he refused to give in to any of their demands, apart from authorizing a new translation of the Bible. For many Puritans this was not enough and some of them thought of leaving England and starting a new life.

THE PILGRIM FATHERS By 1606 some Puritans had decided to set up their own *congregations*, which were separate from the Church.

These congregations were illegal and the people who belonged to them were known as Separatists. In 1607 the members of one congregation in Scrooby in Nottinghamshire tried to flee to Amsterdam to avoid arrest. This first attempt failed, but in 1609 they returned to the Netherlands and settled in Leiden. In 1620, however, the Separatists decided to try and set up an English *colony* in America. A group of them set sail on a ship called the *Mayflower* in September 1620 and reached America 65 days later (see p. 68).

TOWARDS CIVIL WAR The problems with the Puritans grew worse in the reign of James's son, Charles I (1625–1649). Many more Puritans became Members of Parliament and, as their views clashed with his, Charles tried to rule without Parliament. This failed and in 1642 the two sides declared war (see pp. 24–25).

Puritans' Lifestyle

Puritans wanted to live plainly and quietly. They dressed in a simple way. They worked hard, but set Sunday aside as a day of prayer. Puritans had little time for pleasure and tried to ban old customs such as dancing around the Maypole. When Oliver Cromwell became Lord Protector of England in 1653, he even abolished Christmas.

Punishment of Witches

If people who were tried for witchcraft said they were innocent, they were tortured until they confessed, then they were killed. These tortures included being stretched on a rack, being ducked in a pond, and being forced to swallow large amounts of water.

Sometimes people accused of witchcraft were thrown into deep water. If they swam out they were guilty, and were hanged or burned at the stake. Those who were innocent drowned.

Above. Some of the English Protestants who had settled in the Netherlands leaving Delft on their way to join the *Mayflower*.

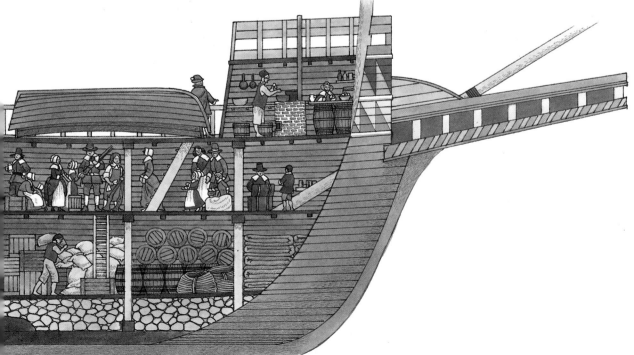

Left. This is a reconstruction of the *Mayflower*, the ship in which the Pilgrim Fathers went to America. They had to take all their provisions with them, including food and fresh water for the journey, plus food for when they arrived. There were no refrigerators and so all the meat had to be smoked or salted to stop it going bad. They also took tools to cut down trees and build cabins to live in, tools for farming and guns so that they could go hunting and defend themselves if necessary.

The Struggle for Power
THE RISE AND FALL OF SPAIN

Spain's rise to power began in the late fifteenth century during the reign of Ferdinand (1479–1516), and Isabella (1479–1504). Their marriage had united the two ancient kingdoms of Castile and Aragon and later they brought Granada and Navarre under their rule as well. Their daughter, Catherine of Aragon, married the English king, Henry VIII (see p. 13). Another daugher, Joanna the Mad, married Philip, Duke of Burgundy, who was the son of Maximilian of Austria, the Holy Roman Emperor. Philip's lands included the Netherlands, where he and Joanna lived and where their son, Charles, was born in 1500.

WAR AGAINST FRANCE When Duke Philip died in 1506, Charles became the ruler of the Netherlands. In 1516 he inherited Spain from Ferdinand and in 1519 he inherited the Holy Roman Empire from Maximilian. King Francis I of France (1515–1547) and Pope Leo X (1513–

1521) both objected to this, as they thought it would make Charles too powerful, but in spite of their protests he was crowned as Emperor Charles V in 1520.

This marked the beginning of a struggle for power between France and Spain which was not finally settled until 1659, although the two countries were not at war all the time. They were at war for most of Charles's reign, however, as both tried to gain power in Italy, which at that time was divided into many *city-states*.

WAR AGAINST THE PROTESTANTS After the Reformation (see pp. 10–11), Charles also had to face the problem of a growing number of Protestants in Germany and in parts of the Netherlands. He hoped to convert them back to Catholicism, but instead the German princes formed a military *alliance* against him, called the Schmalkaldic League. In 1546 Charles V went to war against it. His armies defeated those of the League the

Above. A fiesta in the Plaza Mayor in Madrid in around 1600. Madrid was a small town until Philip II made it the capital of Spain in 1561. He planned it carefully, with wide streets and large squares such as this one. Madrid became a center for art and literature as well as a center of government. By 1600 the rich lived in large houses, but most people lived in slums.

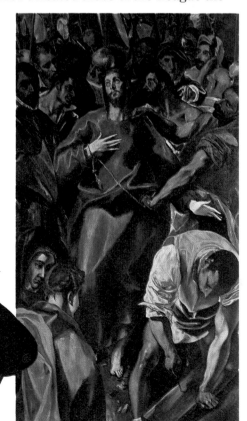

Right. A painting, titled "El Espolio," by Domenikos Theotokopoulos. He was known as El Greco, or "the Greek." He trained as an artist in Venice and later lived in Toledo in Spain.

Below. Charles I of Spain inherited the kingdom of Spain from his grandfather, Ferdinand, in 1516. Four years later he also became Emperor Charles V of the Holy Roman Empire.

following year, but in 1551 two of the German Protestant rulers joined forces with Henry II of France (1547–1559) and made Charles accept their demands.

PHILIP II By 1554 Charles was getting old and tired and so he decided to hand the throne of the Netherlands to his son, Philip. Two years later he also gave Philip the kingdom of Spain and its overseas possessions. Charles then gave the Holy Roman Empire to his own brother, Ferdinand, before retiring to a monastery where he died in 1558.

SPAIN'S GOLDEN AGE Spain reached the height of its power in Philip's reign. In 1559 he signed the Peace of Chateau-Cambrésis, which ended the wars with France over Italy and gave Spain control of Milan, Naples, Sardinia and Sicily. He made Madrid into his capital in 1561. Art and literature flourished. In 1580 Philip took over Portugal and united it with Spain.

SPAIN'S DECLINE Philip's obsession with stamping out heresy led him into costly wars. He intervened in the French Wars of Religion against the Huguenots (see p. 12). He also hoped to turn England and the United Provinces of the Netherlands back to Catholicism and in 1588 he launched his Armada, a great fleet of ships, against them (see pp. 20–21). When he died in 1598, Spain's economy was ruined and the country was almost bankrupt.

Annexation of Portugal

In 1578 King Sebastian of Portugal was killed in battle in Morocco. He had no heirs to succeed him, so a temporary monarchy was set up with Cardinal Henry as king. Cardinal Henry asked the pope to allow him to marry in the hope of starting a new line of Portuguese monarchs, but he died in 1580 before this could happen. Philip II of Spain then claimed the Portuguese throne as he was Sebastian's uncle and nearest relative.

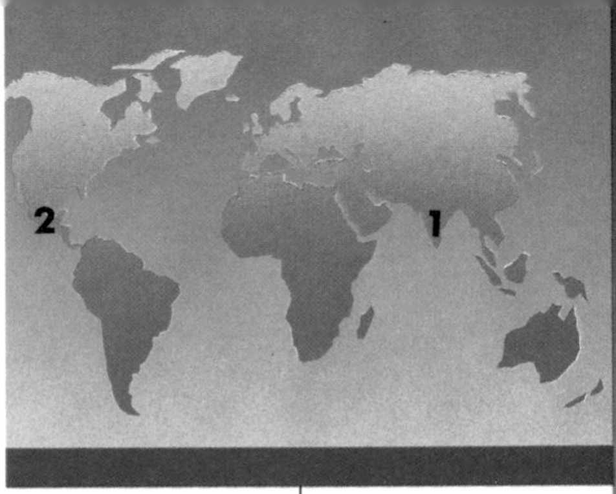

1 In India, Nanak founded the Sikh religion in 1519. He was born in Lahore in 1469 and brought up as a Hindu. He traveled widely in India, visiting both Hindu and Muslim centers. He finally settled in Kartarpur, where he attracted a large number of followers. His new religion combined ideas from both the Hindu and the Muslim faiths.

2 After the Spanish conquest of the Aztecs in Mexico, missionaries set out from Spain to convert the survivors to Roman Catholicism. At first this was often done by force and everything relating to the old religions was destroyed. Later missionaries treated the native population with more respect and encouraged them to talk about their past and continue their culture.

Dynastic Inheritances of Charles V

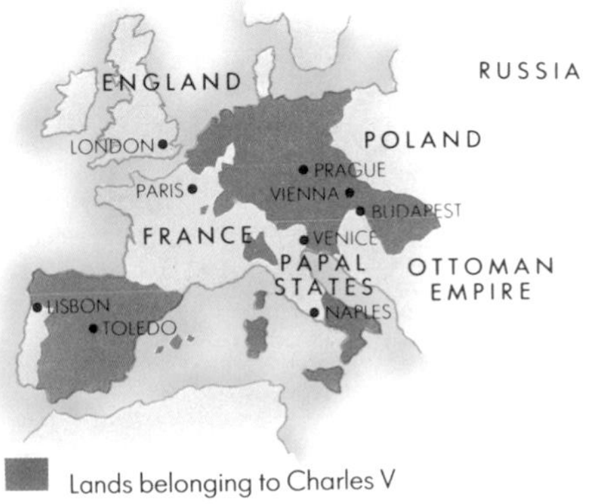

Below. A reconstruction of the Escorial palace which Philip II had built for himself in the hills just outside Madrid. It was built between 1563 and 1584, measures 162 meters by 204 meters and is made of granite. Philip himself probably helped to design it. It is quite a plain design. Apart from its size, it had little of the luxury of other royal palaces of this period.

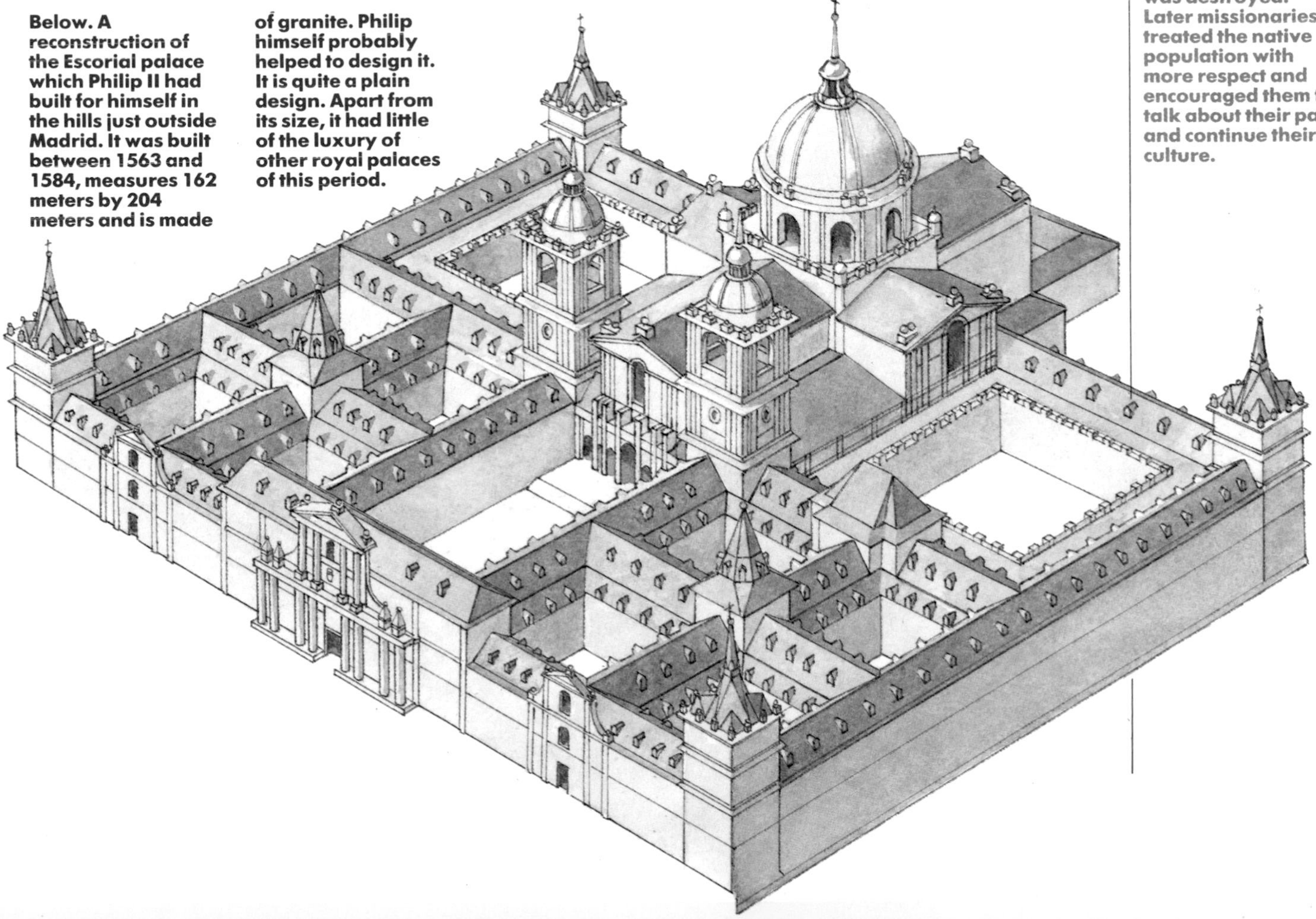

THE SPANISH ARMADA

The Route of the Armada

Left. At this time ships were made of wood and so fire was always a danger, especially if the ships were close together. A fire could easily spread among them.

Above. This map shows the route taken by the Spanish Armada after it left Lisbon on May 30, 1588, up to when it returned there in the autumn of that year.

In the early sixteenth century, Spain and England were allies, but by the 1580s they were enemies. One reason for this was the difference in their religions. Philip II of Spain wanted England to remain a Catholic country after the death of his wife, Mary I, in 1558. When it did not, he supported Mary, Queen of Scots, in her claim to the English throne. Elizabeth I of England had Mary executed in 1587 and also supported the Netherlands in its struggle for independence from Spain. Meanwhile, English ships were also attacking and robbing Spanish treasure ships returning from America. Philip decided to settle all these problems by force and made plans to invade England.

THE INVASION PLAN Philip had an army of around 20,000 men in Spain and another of about 30,000 men in the Netherlands. He thought that the armies together would be able to invade England. He planned to send his army from Spain to the Netherlands on a fleet of ships which became known as the Spanish Armada.

PREPARING THE FLEET Philip needed a great many ships to transport so many men. He also needed warships to defend them from an English attack at sea, and large supplies of weapons and food. Early in 1587 he started to gather all these things together at Lisbon in Portugal, and at Seville and Cadiz in Spain.

THE ATTACK ON CADIZ In May 1587, Philip's plans suffered a great setback when the English sea captain, Sir Francis Drake, raided Cadiz. In the attack Drake and his men destroyed many ships and some of the warehouses where the supplies of weapons and food were stored. This incident became known as "The Singeing of the King of Spain's Beard."

SETTING SAIL The 130 ships of the Armada finally left Lisbon on 30 May 1588. They had been delayed by bad weather and there were more storms as they sailed northwards. On 19 June they had to stop at Corunna for repairs and more supplies. Only 50 ships could get into the harbor and the rest were scattered when another storm blew up that night. It took a month for the Armada to regroup and get ready to sail again.

THE BATTLE The Armada was seen off Cornwall on 29 July and the next day the English fleet sailed out of Plymouth to meet it. The first shots were fired on

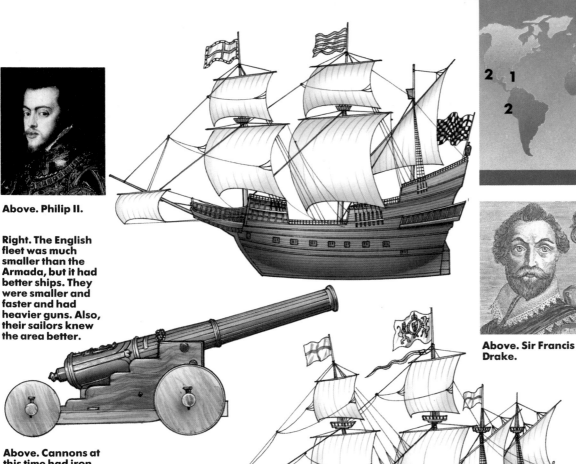

Above. Philip II.

Right. The English fleet was much smaller than the Armada, but it had better ships. They were smaller and faster and had heavier guns. Also, their sailors knew the area better.

Above. Sir Francis Drake.

Above. Cannons at this time had iron barrels and were mounted on wooden frames. They could not fire very far, so enemies had to be quite close before a cannon could do any damage.

Right. Most of the ships were troop-carriers and were slow-moving. They were protected by fighting ships, like the one reconstructed here.

1 Christopher Columbus sailed to the West Indies in 1492 and claimed the islands where he landed for Spain. This was the start of the Spanish conquest of Central and South America. It is estimated that before the conquest the native population was around 25,000,000. By 1580, it was no more than 1,900,000 as a result of ill-treatment, malnutrition and disease spread by the Europeans.

2 In 1545 the Spaniards discovered silver in Peru and Mexico. They forced the native people to work in the mines, but shipped all the silver back to Spain.

3 In 1571 Spain claimed a group of islands and named them the Philippines after Philip II. This gave them a share of the spice trade which had previously been dominated by the Portuguese.

How England Prepared for War

England had been expecting a Spanish invasion, but Elizabeth I was reluctant to spend money on defending the country. The English army fighting the Spanish in the Netherlands had not been paid for months, and there was no army at home. However, Sir John Hawkins persuaded the queen to strengthen the navy.

A system of beacons was also set up on all the hilltops in England, from Cornwall to York. Their fires were lit to warn everyone when the Armada was sighted off the English coast.

31 July, but at first neither side did much damage to the other.

On 1 August the Armada formed into a crescent shape, which was difficult to attack. It headed for Calais, France, near to where it hoped to meet the Spanish soldiers from the Netherlands. The English fleet followed and at midnight on 7 August attacked the Armada with eight *fire ships* while it was at anchor. The Spanish captains panicked and many headed for the open sea. The next day the English fleet took advantage of this by attacking the scattered ships off Gravelines.

THE ARMADA DEFEATED The English ships were easier to maneuver than the Spanish ones and their sailors were more used to the English Channel. They sailed in between the Spanish ships and fired cannons at them from close range. Many Spanish ships were damaged, one sank and two ran aground. Then the wind changed, forcing the Armada into the North Sea.

The English fleet followed as far as Scotland, before it ran out of ammunition. The Armada then sailed right round Scotland and along the west coast of Ireland to get back to Lisbon. The weather was stormy and fewer than half of the ships managed to return home.

THE THIRTY YEARS' WAR

The religious and political conflicts which had divided Europe since the Reformation (see pp. 10–11) came to a head in the Thirty Years' War. This started in 1618 when the Protestant noblemen of Bohemia (in modern-day Czechoslovakia) threw two of their Catholic governors out of one of the windows of a castle in Prague. The noblemen then chose the Protestant Frederick as the next king of Bohemia. Less than a year after Frederick was crowned, however, Ferdinand II became Holy Roman Emperor (1619–1637). Ferdinand wanted to convert his whole empire back to Catholicism. He started by attacking Bohemia.

THE BOHEMIAN WAR, 1618–1627 The Bohemians did not get the help they expected from the Protestant countries of Europe and so in 1620 Ferdinand's army entered Bohemia. It defeated Frederick's army outside Prague and marched triumphantly into the city, while Frederick and his family fled to the Netherlands. Ferdinand's victory was so complete that by 1627 Catholicism was the only religion allowed in Bohemia.

DENMARK JOINS THE WAR, 1625–1629 The Thirty Years' War soon spread to other parts of the empire and involved other countries too. Spain took the side of the Holy Roman Empire and in 1621 fighting broke out between the Spanish and the Dutch in the Rhineland. The Spanish army was the more successful and so in 1625 the Dutch asked Denmark and England for help. The Danes did most of the fighting, but by 1629 they had been defeated. England withdrew from the war and Denmark agreed not to interfere in German affairs again.

SWEDEN JOINS THE WAR, 1630–1634 After the defeat of Denmark, King Gustavus Adolphus of Sweden (1611–1632), "the Lion of the North," felt that the Protestant religion was in danger. Swedish trade was also threatened by the plans of the Spanish Prime Minister, Olivares, to expand Spanish power to the

Left. Gustavus Adolphus, king of Sweden 1611–1632. He was a great soldier and also made reforms in education and administration.

Above. Angry Protestants in the state of Bohemia throwing two of their Catholic governors out of a window of a castle in Prague in 1618.

This became known as the Defenestration of Prague. It led to the start of the Thirty Years' War.

Baltic Sea. These threats led Gustavus to go to war against Spain and the Holy Roman Empire in 1630.

At first the Swedes were successful, defeating the Imperial army at Breitenfeld in 1631. The Swedish army stayed in Germany and in November 1632 won another victory at Lützen.

Gustavus was killed in this battle and his chancellor, Oxenstierna, took command. He was less successful than the king, however, and in September 1634 his army was defeated by the armies of Spain and the Holy Roman Empire at Nordlingen and Sweden withdrew from the war.

Right. This map shows how the Thirty Years' War affected the civilian population. In areas where the fighting was heaviest, some small towns and villages lost more than 50 percent of their inhabitants. Some people simply moved away to a different area, but many died when their towns were besieged or set on fire. Even more died as a result of diseases such as plague and typhus which were spread by the soldiers.

Decreases in Population during the Thirty Years' War

BALTIC SEA

POLAND

NETHERLANDS

BERLIN ● FRANKFURT

● COLOGNE

● PRAGUE

BOHEMIA

HUNGARY

SWITZERLAND

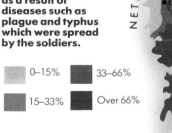

0–15%	33–66%
15–33%	Over 66%

Above. The Battle of Lützen, November 1632. Gustavus Adolphus was killed in the fighting, but his army went on to win the battle.

Above. Cardinal Richelieu, who helped to make France more powerful than Spain.

Treaty of Westphalia

Under this treaty, the Holy Roman Empire lost much of its power. German states such as Saxony, Brandenburg and Prussia became separate countries.

Sweden was given land on the south shore of the Baltic Sea, and France gained Alsace, together with the cities of Metz, Toul and Verdun. The United Provinces of the Netherlands, which had been in revolt against their Spanish rulers since 1568, finally became independent, as did Switzerland.

THE FRENCH PHASE OF THE WAR, 1635–1648 In 1635 the French minister Richelieu decided to take his country into the war against Spain and the Holy Roman Empire. As France was also a mainly Catholic country, this action meant that religion was no longer an important aspect of the war. Instead it had become a continuation of the old conflict between the Habsburgs, who ruled Spain and the Holy Roman Empire, and the Bourbons, who ruled France.

In 1636 part of the Spanish army almost reached Paris, but from 1637 the French and their Protestant allies began to defeat the Spanish. After the French victory at Rocroi in 1643 Olivares fell from power, but another five years passed before there was peace.

THE TREATY OF WESTPHALIA, 1648 The Thirty Years' War was brought to an end by the Treaty of Westphalia in 1648. This treaty gave independence and religious freedom to the United Provinces of the Netherlands, to the Swiss cantons, and to many of the German states which had been part of the Holy Roman Empire. It did not bring peace between the Bourbons and the Habsburgs, however, and the struggle for power between France and Spain continued until 1659.

THE ENGLISH CIVIL WAR

BANCKET HAVS

As this picture shows, the execution of King Charles I took place in the open air and attracted a large crowd of people.

The conflict between the king and the Puritans in Parliament led to civil war in the reign of Charles I (1625–1649). One reason for this was Charles himself. He believed he was king by *Divine Right* and represented God on earth. This convinced him that he was always right and so he only took Parliament's advice when he wanted to. If Parliament disagreed with him, he dismissed it and ruled on his own. As he was always short of money, however, he had to keep calling Parliament back in order to obtain more money through *taxation*, because he could not legally raise taxes without the agreement of Parliament.

THE KING RULES WITHOUT PARLIAMENT Charles's most serious attempt at ruling without Parliament started in 1629. With the help of three ministers, he found ways of raising money without taxation. By 1635 his financial problems were over, so long as England did not become involved in any wars.

REBELLION IN SCOTLAND Charles ruled both England and Scotland, but the two countries had separate governments. Although both countries were Protestant, the Scottish Church had developed along different lines from the English Church. In 1637 Charles tried to make

the people of Scotland use the *English Prayer Book*. They refused and in 1639 they raised an army against him. Charles could not afford to fight a war and so in April 1640 he had to call another Parliament.

THE TENSION INCREASES This Parliament was dismissed after three weeks. Charles was still short of money, so he had to call Parliament again in November, but it seemed impossible to resolve the differences between its Puritan members and the king. Then in October 1641 Charles made peace with the Scots. Before he could dismiss Parliament again, rebellion broke out in Ireland. The Puritans would only give him the money to deal with this rebellion if he allowed Parliament to elect the chief officers of the kingdom. Charles refused and in January 1642 he tried to arrest five Members of Parliament in the House of Commons. He did not succeed, but this act made war unavoidable.

THE COUNTRY AT WAR The first Civil War started on August 22, 1642 and lasted for four years. In that time, fighting took place in many parts of the country. In some places there were pitched battles, as at Edgehill and Marston Moor. In other places towns or castles were besieged. When this happened, normal life was disrupted

1 Mary, Queen of Scots, was born in 1542. She was a Roman Catholic and the grand-daughter of the sister of Henry VIII of England. She became Queen of Scotland when her father, King James V of Scotland, was killed in battle when she was one week old. She spent much of her childhood at the French court and married the future king of France in 1558. When he died in 1561, she returned to Scotland. She was not popular, however, and by 1567 had been forced to give up the throne. She fled to England, where the queen, Elizabeth I, had her imprisoned until 1587 in case she tried to claim the English throne.

2 In the 1580s Sir Walter Raleigh made the first attempts at founding English colonies in North America, but none of them succeeded.

Above. A portrait of the Parliamentarian leader, Oliver Cromwell.

Main Battles and Sieges during the Civil War

Above. The main battles and sieges of the Civil War. Nearly every part of the country was involved at some time between 1642 and 1646. There were many little skirmishes as well as the major battles shown here.

Above left. A Royalist, or cavalier, soldier wore his hair long and curling. On the right is a typical Parliamentarian soldier, also known as a Roundhead because of his short hairstyle. He wore plainer clothes too.

and many people suffered whether they were soldiers or civilians.

No particular group of people supported either side and even families were sometimes divided, with some family members supporting the king and others supporting Parliament. In 1646, however, the Parliamentarian army under Oliver Cromwell (1599–1658) defeated the Royalists and the king was taken prisoner. The first Civil War was over.

THE DEATH OF THE KING Even in prison Charles carried on scheming. He planned a second Civil War, which started in the summer of 1648, but his armies were soon defeated. His actions proved he could not be trusted and on January 20, 1649 he was accused of treason and tried before Parliament. He was found guilty and executed on January 30.

The second Civil War continued until 1651, when Cromwell defeated the army of the dead king's son, who was also called Charles. England was ruled without a monarch until 1660, with Cromwell ruling alone without an elected Parliament from 1653 until his death in 1658, when he was succeeded by his son Richard. Two years later, Charles I's son returned from France and became King Charles II.

The Execution of Charles I

Charles I spent his last night at Whitehall Palace, where he had held many lavish entertainments during his reign. A special scaffold had been built outside the banqueting hall and at 2 o'clock in the afternoon Charles stepped on to it from an open window.

It was a bitterly cold day and so Charles wore two shirts so that he would not shiver and seem frightened in front of the large crowd which had gathered to watch. On the scaffold with him were three shorthand writers who took down his last words. Then he put his head on the block and the executioner cut it off with one blow.

CHANGES IN LAND WARFARE

Although castles were a good means of protection in the Middle Ages, this picture of Raglan Castle in Wales shows that stone walls were no defense against gunpowder.

fight well. In the Thirty Years' War he split them into groups of 500 so that everyone in each group knew what was happening. He also changed the way that battles were fought. At the opening of a battle, he used his *musketeers* and gunners with mobile field-guns to shoot down the *pike-men* at the front of the enemy lines. Then he charged through with the *cavalry* to mow down as many of the enemy as possible with the weight of the attack. He also ignored the traditional battle season, which only lasted through the summer, and was prepared to go on fighting throughout the winter.

Between 1500 and 1650 there were many changes in the way battles were fought on land and in the effect they had on the people involved. One reason for this was the increasing use of *gunpowder*, which made new weapons possible and at the same time meant that castles and fortified houses became useless as a means of defense.

Another reason was the rise of powerful rulers, first of all in France, Spain and England, and later in countries like Sweden and the Netherlands. These monarchs had armies of their own and so, unlike the medieval kings, they did not have to rely on help from private armies raised by rich noblemen in times of crisis.

THE SIZE OF ARMIES At this time, armies were usually quite small. An army of 30,000 men was almost certain to outnumber its enemy, as a force of even 20,000 was thought to be large. When the French fought against the Spanish in Germany in the Thirty Years' War in the early seventeenth century (see pp. 22–23), their largest army only numbered 14,000 men. This meant that most battles were on a fairly small scale.

TACTICS AND DISCIPLINE In the sixteenth century most armies were badly organized and badly disciplined. They did very little drill or practice and often ignored commands on the battlefield.

King Gustavus Adolphus of Sweden (see p. 22) was one of the first to organize his armies so that they could

DISEASE AND INJURY If a soldier in this period was injured, he was far more likely to die of an infection in his wounds than from the wounds themselves. This was because military camps were very unhygienic and nobody understood the need to keep a wound clean. There were no proper army hospitals or trained nurses to look after those who were injured or sick.

A soldier was also more likely to die from disease than be killed in battle. No-one knew how to stop diseases from spreading, and sometimes more than half an army could be wiped out by diseases like plague, typhus and malaria. For example, in 1625 the Duke of Buckingham left England with an army of 12,000 men to fight against the Spanish army in the Netherlands. They had only reached Calais on the French coast when plague broke out and killed 9000 of them. The rest returned home without having fired a shot.

CIVILIAN SUFFERING Wars on land affected the civilian population as well as the armies. If a town was attacked or besieged by an enemy, many of its buildings might be destroyed. Its trade might be disrupted and some of its inhabitants might die of starvation.

People in the countryside did not fare much better. Armies destroyed crops, either accidentally during the course of a battle, or on purpose to stop them falling into enemy hands. Some of the worst civilian suffering of all happened in the Thirty Years' War, which lasted from 1618 to 1648.

Above. Typical soldiers from the sixteenth century rarely wore any sort of a uniform and were not very well organized. They carried a variety of weapons. Some went on foot and some on horseback.

Above. Soldiers in the countryside were not always content just to take crops that were growing in the fields. They often also broke into the farmhouses and attacked the people in them before stealing food and supplies.

Left. Gunpowder was used for handguns as well as for cannons. The guns could only fire one shot before they needed reloading. They were not always reliable and could easily explode, injuring the user instead of his enemy.

More Disciplined Armies

By 1650, armies were becoming more organized. In the Thirty Years' War, Gustavus Adolphus of Sweden had a disciplined army whose soldiers knew who was in command and what they were supposed to be doing.

Oliver Cromwell brought similar ideas to the New Model Army in the English Civil War. His soldiers could be fined for swearing or being drunk. This discipline and organization helped them to win.

Everyday Life
LIVING IN THE COUNTRY

Most people still lived and worked in the countryside, as they had done in the Middle Ages. However, in much of Europe the countryside was slowly changing as the old feudal system disappeared. Many peasants now paid a money rent for their land, instead of having to work for their landlord for two or three days each week. This meant they could work on their own land every day, and this extra work often led to an improvement in the crops and animals they produced. The pattern of land-holding changed, too, as the old *open fields* were reorganized into individual farms. The exception to most of this was France, where the feudal system lasted until the late eighteenth century.

FARMING FOR CASH Many farmers now started to grow more crops than they needed, and to sell the surplus. What they grew depended on where they lived. In southern Europe they grew grapes for wine, and mulberry bushes to feed the silk worms for the expanding silk industry. In colder areas farmers grew flax for the linen industry and also plants to make dyes.

An increasing population meant that more woollen cloth was needed to clothe everybody and so sheep farming was very profitable. In England some landlords evicted their tenants and used the land for sheep farming. This became so great a problem that in 1534 Henry VIII passed a law forbidding anybody to keep more than 2000 sheep.

Owners of châteaux like this one at Chaumont in France were very wealthy and often owned more than one large estate. Most of them spent their money on their own houses and pleasure, rather than doing anything to improve their land and the way it was farmed. The peasants who lived on the estates were little better than slaves.

TIMES OF FAMINE Even though there were improvements in farming, the farmers still could not always produce enough food for everybody. Sometimes diseases killed whole flocks of sheep and cattle, and in northern Europe grain crops such as wheat and barley failed in cold or wet summers. In southern Europe the crops failed when the spring was too dry.

When this happened, some people died of hunger. Many more were weakened by *malnutrition* and then died of diseases such as plague and smallpox. The famines often led to riots, especially where rich people could afford to buy food from another area and poor people could not.

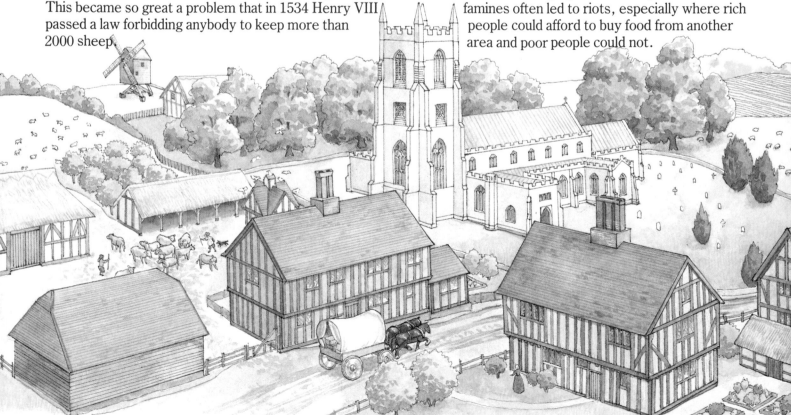

This painting, by the Flemish artist Pieter Brueghel, shows both men and women helping in the fields with the haymaking, while others are carrying baskets of freshly picked fruit and vegetables on their heads. Although agriculture in general was much better organized than it had been in medieval times, most work had to be done by hand. At busy times many people were needed on the farms, but in the winter there was very little work for them to do.

RECLAIMING THE LAND People began to look for ways of making more land available for farming. Most of the forests had already been cleared, but there were still many marshy areas which could be used if they were drained. The pioneers in this work were the Dutch. If an area was below sea-level, they drained it by digging *dykes* around it and pumping the water out into them. Tide-gates, or barriers, built across the dykes then closed automatically when the tide rose and so stopped the water flooding the land.

Charles I of England employed a Dutch engineer, called Vermuyden, to drain much of the land in East Anglia. This upset many local people who had caught fish and water birds on the marshes for a living. These people later turned firmly against the king during the English Civil War (see pp. 24–25).

NOT ENOUGH LAND FOR EVERYBODY By 1500 the population of Europe was back to the size it had been before the Black Death struck in 1347–48. As it started to increase, there was no longer enough land for everyone in the countryside to make a living from farming. Some solved the problem by combining farming with small-scale industry, such as weaving cloth. Many more left the countryside altogether and went to seek their living in a town or city.

As the feudal system disappeared and farming methods became more scientific, the landscape of Europe began to change. Individual farms appeared, surrounded by their own fields and barns. New boundaries were marked out with hedges or walls and in some areas windmills were built to pump the water from low-lying land and make it suitable for farming.

LIVING IN TOWNS

At the beginning of the sixteenth century most European towns were still quite small by modern standards. Even the capital cities like London, Paris and Lisbon counted their populations in thousands and not millions.

THE TOWNS EXPAND Most towns started to grow in this period, partly because the number of births was larger than the number of deaths. People were also moving in from the countryside to find jobs. Those who did, settled down, married and had children to add to the population. The rest joined the growing number of beggars and homeless people, as there was not enough work for everyone. Governments thought that beggars were a threat to the community and passed laws to make life as difficult as possible for them.

THE GREAT FIRE RISK Town streets were usually very narrow and had houses on both sides. Many houses were three or four stories high and each floor jutted out over the one below it. This meant that by the fourth floor, the houses at opposite sides of the street almost touched. This was a great fire risk, as most of the houses were built completely of wood and some also had thatched roofs. If a fire started, whole streets could be destroyed. Because of this, important buildings such as *guild halls* and churches were usually made from stone or brick, which made them less likely to catch fire.

HEALTH AND HYGIENE The overcrowded houses and narrow streets were both health risks. People threw their rubbish into the streets and left it to rot, which attracted rats and other vermin that spread diseases. There were few drains and so pools of stagnant water often gathered in the streets.

Where there were drains and sewers, they were often left open. Nobody understood where diseases came from and so the dirty water was often allowed to flow back into the drinking-water supply, leading to outbreaks of disease, especially during hot summers. The streets were not lit at night and therefore people were also in great danger of being mugged or murdered if they went out after dark.

Shakespeare and the Theater

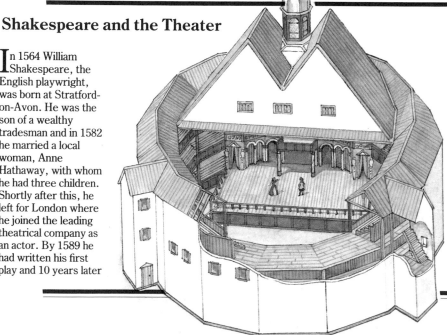

In 1564 William Shakespeare, the English playwright, was born at Stratford-on-Avon. He was the son of a wealthy tradesman and in 1582 he married a local woman, Anne Hathaway, with whom he had three children. Shortly after this, he left for London where he joined the leading theatrical company as an actor. By 1589 he had written his first play and 10 years later he was a shareholder in the newly built Globe Theater in Southwark, on the south bank of the River Thames in London.

Up to this time, many plays had been performed in the courtyards of inns and taverns and this was reflected in the design of the Globe. The stage was in the middle of the circular building. Richer members of the audience sat in galleries all around the stage, while the poorer ones stood in the open area near it.

Although theater-going was very popular in England, the Puritans thought it was not very respectable. All the theaters were closed when Oliver Cromwell came to power.

Most towns at this time were quite small, but very busy. There were often entertainers, like the man and his dancing bear in this picture. Most shopping was done in the open, often from market stalls. Instead of glass windows, shops had wooden shutters which were used as counters by day and covered the window at night.

FASHIONABLE SOCIETY Despite the risks involved in living there, it was fashionable for rich people from the country to have a town house at this time. They often spent the whole winter there. They were more likely to hear the latest news in town and find out about any political intrigues. There was also more entertainment to keep them amused through the winter months.

ENTERTAINMENT Some of the entertainments of this period seem very cruel to us today. For example, people enjoyed watching bear-baiting and cock-fighting. They also enjoyed watching public executions. There were plenty of these as people could be hanged for a great many crimes, including theft or vandalism.

Theatergoing was also popular and there were many street entertainers such as jugglers, acrobats, musicians and men with dancing bears. They traveled from town to town to perform and to entertain people.

The Shambles in York, England, was the street where the butchers had their shops in the sixteenth century. At one point it is so narrow that people can shake hands across the street from the top stories of the houses.

THE BEGINNING OF INDUSTRY

The discovery of how to produce cast iron made it possible to manufacture large objects such as cylinders and gun-barrels, like the ones shown in this picture.

During the sixteenth and seventeenth centuries, industry was beginning to expand in many parts of Europe. It was also becoming better organized. It was still on a very small scale compared with industry today, however. There were very few factories. Instead, most of the work was carried out in people's homes, especially in country districts where farms were not large enough to support a whole family. To earn extra money, the people in these areas worked at such jobs as spinning yarn, weaving cloth and making small metal goods, like iron nails or links for chains. This often involved the whole family, including children as young as four or five.

TEXTILES Cloth-making probably employed more people than any other industry at this time. Most of them worked in their own homes making woolen cloth. The women used a spinning-wheel to turn the raw wool into yarn, which the men wove into cloth on a handloom made mostly of wood. This work was slow, as it took eight women to spin enough yarn for one man to produce one length of cloth.

When the cloth came off the loom, it was taken to the nearest *fulling-mill* to be washed. It might also be dyed. While the cloth was still wet, it was put on a *tenter-frame* in the open air. This helped to stretch the cloth to the required length and width as it dried.

England dominated the cloth trade in the sixteenth century, but its position was challenged by the Netherlands in the seventeenth century. Linen cloth was produced throughout Europe, while silk was produced in France and Italy. By 1650 cotton had been introduced from India and soon became an important textile.

IRON-MAKING For iron ore to turn into metal it has to be smelted. At the beginning of this period, the smelting was done in a *bloomery*, which was little more than a partly enclosed fire, and only produced a few kilograms of iron at a time. The iron contained many impurities, most of which had to be hammered out by a skilled smith.

In the middle of the sixteenth century the first blast furnaces came into use. These were stone structures that could smelt about a ton of iron at a time in a charcoal fire which was totally enclosed. At first, when the furnace was tapped, the molten iron ran out into molds shaped like a sow and her piglets, so it was called pig iron. Later, different shapes of molds were used to cast the iron directly into objects such as cannons and cylinders. It then became known as cast iron.

THE IMPORTANCE OF COAL Coal-mining was also growing in importance, especially in England. The main coalfield was in Northumberland and Durham. Coal from there was carried by sea to London and to other parts of Europe. Much of it was for domestic fires in towns and cities where the local supplies of firewood had been used up. On the banks of the River Tyne, coal was used to heat large pans of seawater to make salt and to heat furnaces to produce glass.

By the end of this period, coal was also being used to supply heat for several other industries, such as brick-making, brewing and pottery. However, it was not used successfully in the iron industry until the early eighteenth century.

Right. The main industrial areas in Europe during this period. In general, areas with good farming land had very little industry. In areas where the land was not good, many families relied on industries such as cloth manufacture, mining and iron-making to provide them with work.

Below. A forge needed iron ore, a good supply of wood for the furnace and water to drive the waterwheel. This wheel worked the bellows for the fire and the trip-hammers to hammer the iron.

Trade and Industry in the Sixteenth Century

■ Major textile areas

■ Major metallurgical areas

SCANDINAVIA

GREAT BRITAIN
DUBLIN
LONDON
NETHERLANDS
AMSTERDAM
ANTWERP
LIÈGE
GERMANY
PRAGUE
ATLANTIC OCEAN
FRANCE
LYONS
MILAN
VENICE
SPAIN
ITALY
GREECE
LISBON
MADRID
NAPLES
GRANADA
PALERMO
MEDITERRANEAN SEA

The Woolen Industry

Many people worked in the woolen industry during this period. Several specialized processes were needed to turn the raw wool into cloth. Most of them had to be done by hand.

The fleeces sheared from the sheep's backs were often tangled, so people had to comb them before the wool was smooth enough to spin into yarn. After being combed, the yarn was still harsh

Above. Women used spinning wheels to make wool into yarn.

and greasy, so once the cloth was woven, it was taken to a fulling-mill. Here the workers washed out the grease and pounded the cloth to make the threads firm and fluffy. When the cloth was dry, another group of people cropped the

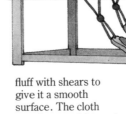

fluff with shears to give it a smooth surface. The cloth was then straightened and pressed.

Above. Men wove the yarn into cloth on looms made mostly of wood. The shuttle was thrown across by hand.

Above. A picture from a book called *De Re Metallica*, by a German called Georgius Agricola, which was published in 1556. It was the first textbook on metal-mining, and was written in Latin and illustrated with many woodcut pictures like this one. Despite his scientific approach to his subject, Agricola was as superstitious as many other people of his time. He warned his readers about the demons that were to be found in some mines.

TRADE AND FINANCE

Above. Sixteenth-century Antwerp was a very busy town. As well as being a center of European trade, it was also an important money market and industrial center. Its population grew from 50,000 in 1500 to 100,000 in 1550.

Although industry was only carried out on a small scale for most of the sixteenth and early seventeenth centuries, it still needed raw materials to make things from and markets to sell the goods when they were completed. This buying and selling was usually conducted by merchants. During the late Middle Ages most of them had been based in Italy, in cities such as Venice, Genoa, Naples and Milan. By 1500, however, other European countries were also becoming important centers of trade. These new centers were to the north and west of Italy and by 1650 they had moved, via Switzerland and Germany, to the Netherlands and Britain.

Left. This is a reconstruction of a typical market-hall. The market officials had their offices upstairs, from where they could see that everything was running smoothly. People who could not afford their own stalls sold their goods in the open area beneath the offices, while richer traders set up their stalls in the market-place.

FAIRS AND MARKETS Much of the trade at this time was carried out at international fairs. One of the largest in the sixteenth century was at Frankfurt in Germany. Here all sorts of goods from many parts of the world were bought and sold. Other markets concentrated on just one product, like woolen cloth, lace or precious metals. Merchants who bought goods at these fairs and markets usually sold them on to shopkeepers to sell to the public

in towns and large villages. The merchants also sold to chapmen—traveling salesmen who went to remote areas, taking with them a selection of small goods, such as ribbons, buttons and laces, to sell to the people living there.

THE MERCHANT ADVENTURERS In 1407 an English company called the Merchant Adventurers was founded

The Areas of Fugger Influence in Europe

▲ Fugger mine
■ Fugger center
● Fugger branch

Above. This painting by Quentin Massys shows an early sixteenth-century Netherlands banker and his wife working together and counting their money. Their clothes are practical and simple and neither of them is wearing any jewelry. This **simplicity, together with a fair amount of equality between men and women in trade and finance, helped to make the Netherlands successful as a trading nation. By the time of the Revolt of the Netherlands against Spain, Amsterdam had overtaken Antwerp** **as the most important trading center of northern Europe. It imported, exported and manufactured goods, as well as providing banking and other financial services.**

Hans Fugger founded the family's business after moving to Augsburg (Germany) in 1367. Its prosperity reached its height in the sixteenth century, led by Jakob Fugger. By that time, the Fuggers controlled the mining of gold, silver and copper in much of central Europe. They had contacts in Venice and Portugal and dominated the port of Antwerp. In the 1530s they had a branch in Chile and by 1587 they also had links with India.

to control the export of woolen cloth from England to Europe. It soon became very powerful. From 1446 to 1567 the company had its center at Antwerp. The center then moved to Hamburg in Germany for 13 years before moving back to the Netherlands.

The most important rivals of the Merchant Adventurers were the traders of the Hanseatic League, which was an association of trading towns in northern Germany. This rivalry often led to trade wars between the two companies and, although they were both still trading in 1650, both companies were dissolved shortly afterwards.

THE RISE OF THE NETHERLANDS As it was quite close to England by sea and had access by rivers to much of continental Europe, the Netherlands was in an ideal position to become a great trading nation. By the middle of the sixteenth century Amsterdam had become its main trading center, handling both goods and finance. This success in trading was one of the reasons which led the United Provinces of the Netherlands to declare their

independence from Spain in 1579, although the Spanish did not accept their independence till 1648.

THE FUGGER FAMILY Several families made a fortune out of manufacturing and trading at this time. Some went on to start early forms of banks, lending money to monarchs and statesmen as well as to other businessmen and merchants. One of the best-known was the Fugger family from Germany, whose business was founded by Hans Fugger, a weaver, in the late fourteenth century. By the sixteenth century his grandson, Jakob Fugger, had also gained mining interests in Europe and acted as the pope's banker. In 1519 he used his money and influence to back Charles V's election as Holy Roman Emperor (see p. 18).

After Jakob's death, the family fortunes declined. One of its members, Anton Fugger, went *bankrupt* in 1550 and caused financial chaos in parts of Europe. Despite this, the business kept going for another 100 years and was not dissolved until the middle of the seventeenth century.

The World of Learning
EDUCATION AND SCIENCE

As a result of the Renaissance, many more people in the sixteenth century wanted to be educated. They wanted to learn ancient languages, such as Greek and Latin, and to study subjects like mathematics and law, as well as religion and *philosophy*. Because of this growing interest in education, many new universities were founded in the sixteenth century and many old ones expanded.

GOING TO UNIVERSITY University education was only for the sons of the rich. Girls were not allowed to study there at all and poor people could not afford to. The son of a rich family might go to university when he was only 10 years old, however. He might study at one university for a year or so and then move on to another. Most of the teaching was done in Latin and so an English boy could study in France, Germany or Italy without learning any

Above. The university at Heidelberg in Germany was founded in 1386. It was one of the many European universities which expanded during the sixteenth century.

Above. Leonardo da Vinci (1452–1519) trained as an artist in Florence, but was also an engineer, designer and scientist. He was interested in anatomy, botany and geology, and worked in France as well as Italy.

Left. Copernicus studied mathematics and music at Cracow and Bologna. He then began to calculate the positions of the planets and thought this would be easier if he pretended that the earth moved around the sun. Then he realized that this was what actually happened.

Above. At this time the Roman Catholic Church taught that the earth was the center of the universe and that the sun, the planets and the stars revolved around it. Copernicus proved this was wrong, but the Church condemned his findings. In 1632 Galileo published a book called

Dialogue on Two World Systems, which looked at the two different views of the universe and supported Copernicus's view. As a result, he was accused of heresy. This picture shows one of his appearances before the Inquisition in Rome in 1633.

modern foreign languages.

In the early sixteenth century, it was also possible to go through university without learning to read or write. This was because there were very few books. The teacher usually had the only copy. He read out loud from it and his students had to learn his words by heart. The examinations were oral, not written, and so some students graduated without ever writing a word.

EDUCATION FOR THE NOT-SO-RICH
The sons of merchants, tradespeople and small landowners usually went to *grammar schools* in the towns where they lived. There they learnt Latin grammar, scripture and a little arithmetic. Girls were taught at home. They learnt needlework, dancing and how to look after the house.

In contrast, poor children never went to school at all. Instead, they helped their parents in the home or at work from the moment they were old enough to be useful.

THE GROWTH OF SCIENCE
Many Renaissance scholars studied the works of the ancient Greeks and Romans. From them they learnt to observe what was happening in the natural world, instead of just accepting what they were told. They carried out scientific experiments and studied plants and animals, as well as human beings.

Medicine and Surgery

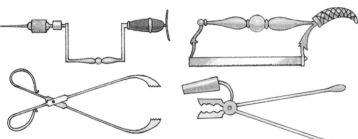

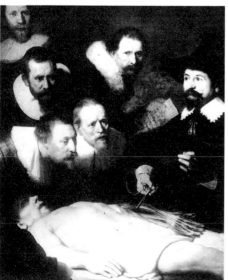

In the sixteenth century, nobody knew much about the human body or about diseases. Some medicines were made from herbs, but others used substances that did more harm than good.

Operations were carried out by barber-surgeons who had few qualifications. Using primitive instruments (some of which are shown above) and no painkillers, they did everything from pulling out teeth to chopping off poisoned legs.

THE CLASH WITH THE CHURCH
This new interest in science brought some people into conflict with the teachings of the Church. One of the first to realize this was Nicolaus Copernicus (1473–1543), a Polish *astronomer* who was also a priest in Germany. His calculations proved that the earth revolved around the sun. This was the opposite of what the Church taught, however, and so Copernicus dared not publish his work until the year he died. His theory was later supported by the work of the Italian scientist, Galilei Galileo (1564–1642).

When the Church heard of this, Galileo was accused of *heresy*. Under pressure from the *Inquisition* in 1632, he had to take back his views. He was at first put in prison, and was then placed under house arrest until his death.

DISCOVERIES AND INVENTIONS
Despite threats from the Church, the scientists continued their experiments. The English physician William Harvey (1578–1657) published his findings on the circulation of blood in the body, while the Dutch physicist Cornelius Drebbel built the first working submarine. Other inventions from this time include the *barometer*, the dredger, the telescope and the watch.

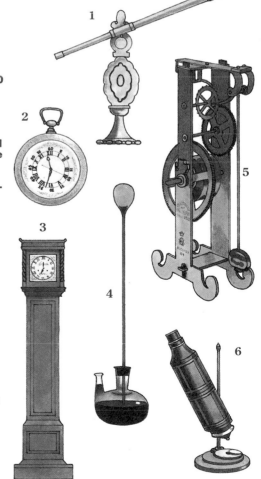

Right. These are reconstructions of some inventions from this period. Peter Hele, or Henlein, invented the watch (2) in 1510 in Germany. He found that if he wound up a strip of springy wire, it would try and straighten itself and this energy could be used as the driving force for a watch. Then came the long-case clock (3), in which the spring was wound up with weights on a chain, and more complicated clockwork (5), used to drive big clocks on churches and other buildings. Lippershey and Jansen made the first microscope (6) in the Netherlands in the 1590s. Lippershey also made the first telescope (1) in 1608. In 1643 Torricelli invented a simple barometer (4), while he was trying to make a suction pump to raise water up for more than 10 meters.

THE SPREAD OF IDEAS

Above. This is Gutenberg's 42-line Bible. Each page had two columns of text and each column was 42 lines long. Before printing was invented, books were written out by hand, like the one shown on the left. Monks did much of this work and it could take months to produce a book.

Traveling from one place to another was difficult in the sixteenth century. Most roads were so bad that people who had to use them traveled on horseback or on foot, rather than in wheeled vehicles. Merchants used strings of *packhorses* to transport many of their goods, while heavy loads went by boat on rivers and lakes whenever possible. In spite of these problems, many people managed to travel long distances.

IDEAS SPREAD BY WORD OF MOUTH Pilgrims, nuns and clergymen made journeys to Rome and other religious centers. Merchants traveled to trading centers like Antwerp and Amsterdam in the Netherlands, and to the cities of northern Italy. Teachers went from one university to another and monarchs sent royal messengers to all parts of their kingdoms. As the old *feudal system* began to disappear in many parts of Europe, country people were able to travel outside their villages without asking for permission. When they bought or sold goods at local markets and fairs, they talked to the people they met. They discussed new ideas and what was going on in the world about them, just as the

merchants and *pilgrims* did with the people they met on their travels. When they got home, they told their families and friends about what they had seen and heard and so the ideas passed on from one place to another without having to be written down.

PRINTED BOOKS For those who could read, the increasing use of printing made the spread of ideas much simpler. Although some books had been printed before the middle of the fifteenth century, they had been very rare and expensive. This was because a whole page of type at a time had to be cut or engraved into a block of wood or metal, and so the block could only be used for that one page.

A German printer called Johann Gutenberg (c. 1400–1468), however, invented a system of printing which used movable type. In this system, a page of type was made up of individual letters which were each cut into a separate piece of metal. When that page had been printed, the type could be rearranged and used for another page. Gutenberg's first printed book appeared in 1455.

PRINTING AND SCIENCE Gutenberg's invention was soon copied in other European countries. This encouraged people to write about their scientific discoveries and during the sixteenth century books were published on subjects such as agriculture, geology, geography, surgery, anatomy, zoology and botany. Other people published plays, poetry and books about travel.

POLITICS AND RELIGION As printing became more widely used, many books and pamphlets on politics and religion were published. These helped to change the way people thought about life and sometimes led to conflict with the state as well as with the Church. Many Bibles were also printed in this period. At first they were all in Latin, as this was the language used by the Roman Catholic Church. After the Reformation (see pp. 10–11), however, Bibles for Protestants were translated into the language of the country where they were going to be read.

Key Dates in the Development of Printing

c.105   Tsai Lun invents paper in China.

700s   Chinese prisoners pass the knowledge on to Arabs; it eventually reaches Europe.

c.1045   Pi Sheng, a Chinese printer, makes the first movable type, using a separate piece of clay for each character. Because the Chinese language has so many characters, it is easier to print a page at a time from a block of wood.

1370–1400   Europeans discover how to print with wooden blocks. A paper-mill is set up in the German states.

1430s   Gutenberg starts printing with movable type.

1476   William Caxton sets up first printing press in England.

1539   First printing shop in North America set up in Mexico City.

1639   Stephen Daye and his son set up a printing press in Cambridge, Massachusetts— the first in the American colonies.

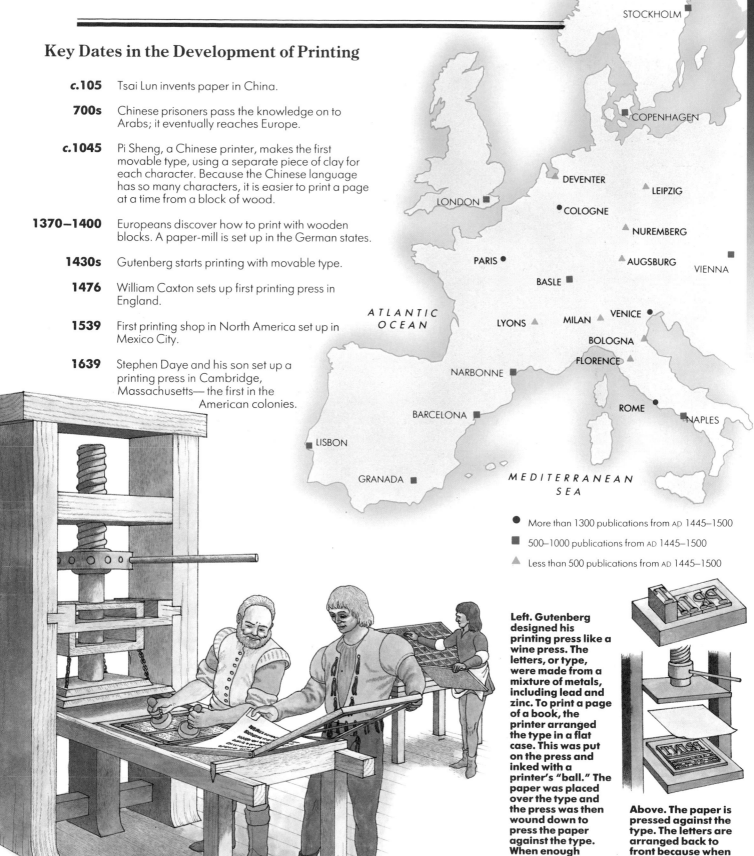

- ● More than 1300 publications from AD 1445–1500
- ■ 500–1000 publications from AD 1445–1500
- ▲ Less than 500 publications from AD 1445–1500

Left. Gutenberg designed his printing press like a wine press. The letters, or type, were made from a mixture of metals, including lead and zinc. To print a page of a book, the printer arranged the type in a flat case. This was put on the press and inked with a printer's "ball." The paper was placed over the type and the press was then wound down to press the paper against the type. When enough copies had been printed, the type was removed and separated into individual letters.

Above. The paper is pressed against the type. The letters are arranged back to front because when their image is transferred to the paper, they will appear the other way around.

Conflicts in Europe
TIME CHART

AD	FRANCE AND SPAIN	BRITAIN	REST OF EUROPE
1500		Wynken de Worde sets up his printing press in Fleet Street, London. This street will be a center of publishing for almost 500 years	
1517			Martin Luther starts the Reformation in Wittenberg, Germany
1519			Death of Leonardo da Vinci, one of the most important artists of the Renaissance
1520	King Charles I of Spain is crowned Emperor Charles V of the Holy Roman Empire. War breaks out between Spain and France		
1523		The first manual on farming is published	
1534		King Henry VIII breaks with the pope. He sets up a church in England with himself as the head	Ignatius Loyola founds the Society of Jesus—the Jesuits
1543			Nicolaus Copernicus, a Polish astronomer, publishes his theory that the earth moves around the sun
1545			First meeting of the Council of Trent to decide on how to reform the Catholic Church
1547			Michelangelo becomes chief architect of St. Peter's in Rome
1554		The future King Philip II of Spain marries Queen Mary I of England	
1558	England loses Calais to the French		
1559	The Peace of Chateau-Cambrésis brings a temporary halt to the conflict between France and Spain		
1560	Death of Henry II of France. His widow, Catherine de' Medici, acts as regent until 1574	The first Puritans appear in England	
1561	Philip II of Spain makes Madrid his capital. Construction starts on the palace of El Escorial		
1564		Birth of William Shakespeare, the playwright	
1562>1598	The Wars of Religion are waged in France		
1568	The start of the revolt by Dutch Protestants against the rule of Philip II of Spain		
1577			Peter Paul Rubens is born in Westphalia. He was to become the greatest Baroque artist
1588	Philip II launches the "Invincible Armada" against England		
1603		James VI of Scotland becomes James I of England on the death of Elizabeth I	
1605	In Spain the novelist Miguel de Cervantes publishes Part One of *Don Quixote*		
1609			Galileo, an Italian scientist, designs a telescope
1618>1648			The Thirty Years' War
1620		A group of Puritans leaves England to avoid persecution and sets up a colony in America	
1629	Cardinal Richelieu becomes Chief Minister to Louis XIII of France		
1642		The English Civil War starts	
1649		King Charles I is executed. England is ruled by a Protector for the next 11 years	

NORTH
AMERICA

ATLANTIC
OCEAN

CENTRAL
AMERICA

SOUTH
AMERICA

EUROPE

AFRICA

ASIA

PACIFIC
OCEAN

INDIAN
OCEAN

AUSTRALIA

PART TWO

Opening up the World

As the Europeans escaped from the narrow views of the Middle Ages, they began to show an interest in the world beyond their own boundaries. Part of this interest was simply curiosity and a desire for more knowledge, but there were other, more important reasons behind the great voyages of discovery in the late fifteenth and early sixteenth centuries.

TRADE The most important reason was the search for new trading routes to the Far East, where luxury goods such as spices and rich materials like brocades came from. Before 1453 these goods had come overland to the markets of the Byzantine Empire, based at Constantinople (modern-day Istanbul), and were then transported to markets further west by merchants who sailed the Mediterranean. In 1453, however, the Ottoman Turks conquered Constantinople and made it the center of a Muslim empire which controlled all the overland routes to the Far East. This gave them a *monopoly* on the spice trade, which the Europeans wanted to break.

In their search for new routes, the European explorers came across some lands which were sparsely populated. This was especially true in North America, where the native population was quite small and spread out. To people who felt oppressed or restricted by life in Europe, these places offered the chance to start a new life and many people went to the New World to escape religious persecution in Europe.

After the Counter-Reformation (see pp. 14–15), many Catholic missionaries also set out for other parts of the world. They hoped to find other Christians, as well as to convert people from other beliefs which they regarded as *heathen*.

DIFFERENT LANDS The world the Europeans found was different from what they had expected. Except for Russia, there were either very few Christians, or none at all. Some countries, such as China, had a more advanced civilization than Europe and so were not impressed by these new visitors.

Other people were still living in the Stone Age, without the benefit of the horse, the wheel or metal tools. This included all the Indians of the Americas, and yet the Inca Empire of South America looked after the old, the young and the sick in a way which Europe would not equal for over 400 years.

The first modern explorers sailed from Portugal and Spain. They were soon joined by the English, the French and the Dutch. By 1650, these countries had sent explorers right around the world and had begun to divide it into new empires for themselves.

THE FIRST WAVE OF EUROPEAN EXPLORATION

In the last quarter of the fifteenth century European explorers began to look for new ways of traveling to India and the Far East, so that they could deal directly with the producers of spices and other luxury items. In the past these goods had either been sent overland to Byzantine markets, or had come from India via the Red Sea and Alexandria. Now, however, both these routes were in the hands of the Muslims, who were thought of as enemies by the Catholic monarchs of Spain and Portugal. Because of this, both kingdoms were willing to support expeditions to find new routes.

THE PORTUGUESE EXPLORERS From the early fifteenth century onwards, the Portuguese had been sailing further and further south along the coast of Africa in search of gold, spices and slaves. In 1487 Bartolomeu Dias sailed round the Cape of Good Hope and into the Indian Ocean before turning back. Vasco da Gama followed his route and reached Calicut in India in 1498. In 1500, Pedro Alvarez Cabral left Lisbon to make the same journey as Vasco da Gama. On the way he landed by chance on the coast of Brazil and claimed it for Portugal, before going on to India.

THE SPANISH EXPLORERS By the late fifteenth century most Europeans knew that the earth was round, not flat, and in 1492 an Italian sailor called Christopher Columbus (c. 1451–1506) convinced the king and queen of Spain that Asia could be reached by sailing westwards from Europe. He left Spain with three ships on August 3 that year and, after reaching the Canary Islands on September 6, he next made landfall on October 12 at San Salvador in the Bahamas. Having over-estimated the size of Asia and under-estimated the size of the earth, Columbus was convinced he had reached India. He still thought this when he died in 1506, even though by that time he had made three more voyages to the New World and claimed all the places where he landed for Spain.

Spanish explorers followed his route to become the first Europeans to set foot on other islands in the West Indies, the mainland of South America and Mexico, and parts of North America.

OTHER EUROPEAN EXPLORERS While the Spanish sailed west and the Portuguese sailed southeast, other Europeans looked for a northwest passage to Asia and then for a northeast one. In 1497 John Cabot and his crew became probably the first Europeans to see Newfoundland since the Vikings had been there in the eleventh century, while in 1553 Willoughby and Chancellor sailed round the North Cape and reached Archangel in Russia. Jacques Cartier (see p. 69) journeyed from France to Canada three times between 1534 and 1541 and explored the east coast and the St. Lawrence River. A new sea-route to Asia was never found, but several countries were newly opened up for settlement and trade.

NAVIGATION The ships that the explorers used were only small and were often at the mercy of the wind and the currents. To find their way, they had to rely on a compass and on observations, made with a *sea-astrolabe*,

Tools of Navigation

The explorers of this period had only very simple equipment to help them navigate. The simplest of all was the compass, which would always point to magnetic north and allowed them to work out which direction they were sailing in.

To find out where they were, sailors had to find their latitude by using an astrolabe and charts that showed the positions of the stars in relation to the earth. They could find their approximate longitude by calculating how fast the ship was traveling in an hour and multiplying this by the number of hours which had passed since they left a known point.

Above. Using a cross-staff, a sailor could work out how far north or south he was by checking the position of the stars.

Above. This astrolabe was used to measure the height of the midday sun.

Above. A compass like this one told the sailor which direction he was sailing in.

Preparing for a Journey

Above. Jacques Cartier visited Canada between 1534 and 1541. Left, John Cabot went to Newfoundland in 1497. Right, Christopher Columbus landed in the Bahamas in 1492.

Exploration Routes 1497–1644

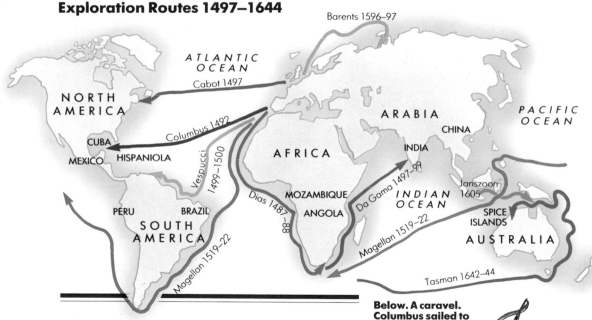

Barents 1596–97

ATLANTIC OCEAN

Cabot 1497

NORTH AMERICA

Columbus 1492

CUBA

MEXICO   HISPANIOLA

Vespucci 1499–1500

AFRICA

ARABIA

CHINA

INDIA

PACIFIC OCEAN

Dias 1487–88

MOZAMBIQUE

Da Gama 1497–99

INDIAN OCEAN

Janszoon 1605

ANGOLA

PERU   BRAZIL

SOUTH AMERICA

SPICE ISLANDS

AUSTRALIA

Magellan 1519–22

Magellan 1519–22

Tasman 1642–44

Left. This map shows some of the routes followed by European explorers between 1487 and 1553.

Below. A caravel. Columbus sailed to America in a ship like this.

Before he could sail, an explorer had to raise money to buy ships and supplies. These included as much food and fresh water as possible, as nobody knew when the ship might reach another port. For the crew, he had to find good sailors who were also very brave and prepared to be away from home for as long as two or three years.

The explorer himself prepared by studying whatever charts and written accounts were available. Often, however, he and his men would be the first Europeans to try the route and so there was nothing to guide him.

of the height of the sun above the horizon at midday or the position of the Pole Star at dusk. With the help of mathematical tables, the sailor could then work out his *latitude*. He could only make a rough estimate of his *longitude*, however, based on the distance he had sailed in a given time. If the sky was clouded over for any length of time, the calculations could not be made accurately and ships often missed their intended destinations. For example, the Pilgrim Fathers (see p. 68) reached Cape Cod when they were trying to get to Virginia. Another group heading for Virginia found themselves instead in Bermuda when they were shipwrecked there.

INTERNATIONAL TRADE

Overseas Trade 1600–1700

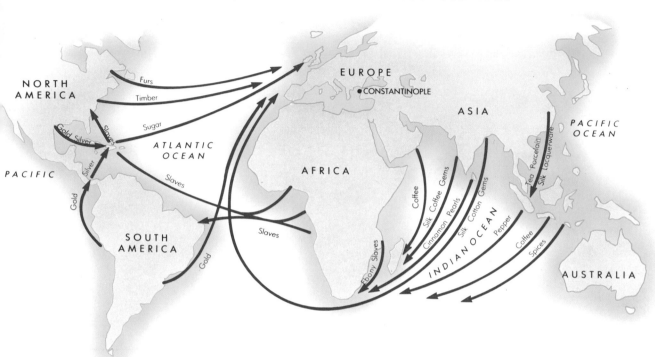

NORTH AMERICA

EUROPE
• CONSTANTINOPLE

ASIA

PACIFIC OCEAN

PACIFIC

ATLANTIC OCEAN

Furs
Timber
Sugar
Gold Silver
Slaves
Silver
Gold
Slaves

AFRICA

Slaves
Gold

SOUTH AMERICA

Slaves

Coffee
Silk Coffee Gems
Cinnamon Pearls
Silk Cotton Gems
Ebony Slaves

Tea Porcelain
Silk Lacquerware

Pepper
Coffee
Spices

INDIAN OCEAN

AUSTRALIA

International trade was well established by 1500. Silks and brocades came overland from China to the Mediterranean coast and then into Europe. On the east coast of Africa, Arabian merchants traded with India, China and the African countries. European countries traded with each other, and also obtained spices and luxury goods from India and the Far East. When the Ottomans took control of the spice trade, Europeans began to look for routes to trade directly with spice-producing countries. Once they found these routes, trade began to change and by 1650 the Europeans were starting to control it.

By the sixteenth century the countries of Europe needed a two-way trade with the rest of the world. As well as wanting to import spices and luxury goods, they also wished to find markets for their own products. This became even more important as the century went on and European industry expanded to produce more goods than were needed at home. Overseas markets had to be found where these goods could be sold for money or traded for something which Europe could not produce.

WHY EUROPE NEEDED SPICES During this period many cattle were killed for meat at the beginning of autumn because the farmers did not have enough foodstuffs to feed all the herd through the winter. There were no refrigerators and so often meat had started to go bad before it was eaten. The only way to keep it fit to eat for any length of time was by salting it, but so much salt had to be used that the meat tasted of nothing else. To make it taste better, people added spices such as pepper, ginger and cinnamon when they were cooking the meat.

THE SPICE TRADE As spices only grew in hot countries, they had to be transported over long distances. Each

When the Europeans visited the New World, they found many plants which they had never seen before, including bananas, pineapples, coconuts, maize and tobacco. They also found tomatoes and potatoes, which they took back to Europe with them. At first they grew potato plants for decoration only, but later they became a very important food crop in several European countries.

Left. The Spanish controlled the production of cochineal. It was used as a red dye and came from the dried bodies of insects that lived on a cactus in Mexico.

Below. In 1576 Ivan IV of Russia sent these merchants and noblemen to Austria. They took furs with them in the hope of setting up trading links between the two countries.

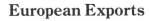

European Exports

Woolen cloth was the main European export in this period. At first it was quite thick to suit colder climates. As trade increased with warmer countries, people tried finer yarns to make less bulky cloth. This was perfected in the seventeenth century.

Another important export was iron. This was first traded in the form of iron bars. Later it was made up into different items before it was exported, as this meant that the Europeans could make more profit from it.

merchant who handled them wanted to make a profit, and when that was added to the cost of bringing the spices to Europe they became very expensive. When the Portuguese reached India, they were able to buy some of these spices directly. This cut their costs and also encouraged them to sail on to find the Moluccas, or Spice Islands (now part of Indonesia). The king of Portugal then claimed a monopoly on the spice trade. This did not last very long, however, as other European explorers found different routes to the Spice Islands and India and also began to trade directly with them.

LUXURY GOODS AND NECESSITIES Besides spices, the European traders were also looking for other luxury goods. For instance, as their own continent became more and more cultivated, there were fewer wild animals to be hunted for their skins. As rich people still wanted furs, these had to be brought from overseas. When Richard Chancellor went to Russia in 1553 and set up the Muscovy Company, the fur trade was one of the things he was most interested in. Similarly, when Samuel de Champlain explored Canada in 1608 he started a trade in furs for France (see p. 69).

The Europeans were also interested in obtaining brocades and tea from China, silks and printed cottons from India, and unusual foods, such as pineapples, from the New World.

Not all trade was in luxury goods, however. As Europe used up all its own tall trees for building houses and ships, timber began to be imported from America. Harvest failure was always a possibility in Europe, too, and so grain was sometimes imported to be sold at a high price in times of famine.

THE THREATS TO TRADE Trading with countries overseas was always a risky business. Apart from the constant threat of wars, storms and shipwrecks, there was also a danger from pirates who might capture the ship and steal its cargo. Because of all these risks, wise merchants invested their money in several different ships and each ship had a number of owners. Thus, if the ship and its cargo did not reach their planned destination, the loss was spread among several merchants and they were all able to carry on trading. Despite the risks, some merchants became very rich and were able to buy large town houses and even country estates.

COLONIZING DISTANT LANDS

The Portuguese built Fort Jesus near Mombasa in Kenya in the late sixteenth century to protect their trading routes to East Africa and India.

When the Europeans began their voyages of discovery in the late fifteenth century, they were looking for new trade routes. As they found these, they began setting up permanent trading posts in the countries they were trading with, and they soon grew into European colonies. In many countries the traders from Portugal and Spain were soon followed by missionaries, who hoped to convert the local populations to Catholicism. In some countries the colonies outgrew their original purpose and Europeans who were not traders moved to live there.

COLONIES THAT FAILED Not all the attempts at building colonies were successful. In some countries the Europeans were turned out and the frontiers were closed against them. This happened in Japan, even though the Europeans had been welcomed there at first. In China the situation was even worse because the Chinese thought the Europeans had nothing to offer them and looked on their methods of trading as a form of piracy. By the 1550s, they allowed Portuguese traders onto the waterfront at Macao, but would not let them go any further.

AFRICA The Europeans had more success in Africa, where the Portuguese set up some of the earliest trading colonies along the coast. By 1600 there were Portuguese colonies at Luanda on the west coast, and at Butua, Matapa, Mozambique, Kilwe, Mombasa and Malindi on the east, but the interior of the continent remained a mystery.

THE SPANISH IN AMERICA The Spaniards soon realized the wealth of the new lands they had reached and set about exploiting them to the full. In the West Indies they took the land from the Arawak and Carib Indians (see pp. 70–71), who were there when the Spaniards arrived, and turned the Indians into slaves. They did the same to the Aztecs in Mexico and the Incas in South America (see pp. 66–67).

TREASURES FROM AMERICA The Aztecs and the Incas did not use metal for making tools. They did use vast amounts of both gold and silver for making ornaments and statues, however. When the Spaniards found this, they melted all these down into *ingots* and shipped them back to Spain. There the precious metals were used to pay for the wars being fought against other European powers and also to buy other goods in Europe to trade with the New World. When this supply of gold and silver ran out, the Spaniards discovered silver at various sites in Mexico and South America. They forced the Indians to mine these sites and, when most of the Indians had died from diseases and ill-treatment, the Spaniards replaced them with slaves from Africa.

THE EUROPEANS IN NORTH AMERICA The colonization of North America happened later than that of South America and Mexico. Although Verrazzano sailed along the east coast of North America in 1524 and Cartier explored the St. Lawrence River in 1536, both claiming these lands for France, no serious attempts at colonizing were made until the 1580s.

At this point an English explorer, Sir Walter Raleigh, tried to establish some English colonies in an area he called Virginia, but none of them survived. A more successful attempt was made in 1607 when Jamestown was founded and this encouraged other settlers to follow. These settlers had a little more respect for the American Indians than the Spanish had, but they still forced the native peoples off the land which had been theirs for generations. Many Indians also died from diseases brought to America by the Europeans.

Right. Jamestown was the first successful English colony in America, but the early years were very difficult for the settlers. The climate and soil were wrong for the seeds they brought with them. Many people died of famine and disease. Then one of their leaders discovered how to grow maize and grind it into flour. Another man found out how to grow tobacco and this was traded in England in return for farm tools and other essential goods.

Problems of Colonization

When people first started to try and colonize the land which Sir Walter Raleigh had called Virginia, they ran into many problems.

At the end of a long and often dangerous sea journey, they had to try and make homes for themselves in unknown territory before the winter set in. They had to clear the land of trees and make them into houses and furniture. They also had to find a reliable water supply and try to gather or grow enough food to last until the spring, as the ships they had arrived on were not big enough to allow them to bring many supplies from England.

All these efforts failed, and many of the early colonists died in America from a combination of the cold weather, disease and malnutrition.

European Possessions c. 1650

NORTH AMERICA

EUROPE

ASIA

JAMESTOWN

ATLANTIC OCEAN

AFRICA

GOA

PACIFIC OCEAN

TENOCHTITLAN

MALINDI

MOMBASA

INDIAN OCEAN

JAVA

LIMA

SOUTH AMERICA

LUANDA

KILWA

RIO DE JANEIRO

MOZAMBIQUE

JAMESTOWN

Portuguese

French

Spanish

Dutch

British

Above. Some of the places that were colonized by Europeans in the sixteenth and seventeenth centuries. Many colonies were set up for trade. Others were set up as places for people from Europe to settle as farmers and merchants. This usually involved taking land from the native peoples and destroying a way of life they had followed for centuries.

Right. Sir Walter Raleigh.

Right. This woodcarving shows a plan of the Dutch trading colony in Nagasaki harbor in Japan. Dutch merchants started trading with the Japanese in 1567 and at first they were welcomed. However, in the early seventeenth century the Japanese wanted to end all contact with foreigners. All Europeans were banished, apart from a few Dutch merchants. Even they had to keep to this one small island.

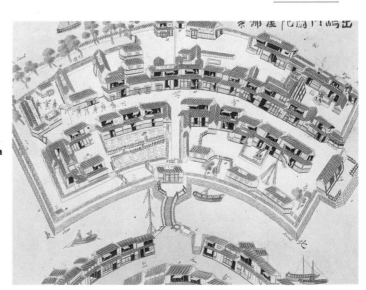

EXPLORING THE PACIFIC OCEAN

Above. The Portuguese navigator Ferdinand Magellan using an astrolabe on board his ship. Because most artists had no idea of what lived in the oceans, they added creatures like mermen and sirens to their pictures.

The greatest problem for adventurers wanting to explore the Pacific Ocean was the lack of an accurate method of navigation. The astrolabe and the *quadrant* worked well enough for finding the way to a large area of land, but were not much use in the Pacific Ocean where there were so many small islands. One of these islands might be sighted on one voyage and then not seen again for many years, as they could not be marked accurately on a chart. Because of this, no serious attempts were made to explore the ocean itself until the middle of the seventeenth century, although it was crossed several times by navigators looking for a southwest route to the Spice Islands. The Spanish conquistadors also sailed north and south across the Pacific along the coast of America.

FERDINAND MAGELLAN The Portuguese navigator Ferdinand Magellan (*c.* 1480–1521) gave the Pacific Ocean its name. He also led the first expedition to sail right around the world. Magellan was supported by the king of Spain, who gave him a fleet of five ships to go in search of a western route to the East Indies. He left Seville in September 1519 and reached the Pacific Ocean in November 1520. After 98 days' sailing, he arrived in the Philippines. Soon afterwards, Magellan was killed in a local dispute and Juan Sebastian del Cano took command. He crossed the Indian Ocean, visited Mozambique and arrived back in Seville with just one ship in September 1522. He and his crew had circumnavigated the world.

Their route was later followed by others, including Sir Francis Drake from England.

THE PHILIPPINES Although Magellan reached the Philippines in 1521, they were not conquered by Spain until 1571. Even then the Spanish influence was mainly on the coast, and Muslims, called "Moros" by the Spaniards, kept them off the islands of Mindanao and Sulu. The Philippines became a trading center, with Chinese *junks* carrying porcelain and silks to Manila to be traded for silver from Mexico.

THE DUTCH EAST INDIA COMPANY Because of their struggle for independence from Spain, the Dutch were forbidden to trade for spices in Lisbon. They therefore decided to break the Portuguese and Spanish monopoly by trading directly with the spice-producing countries, and in 1602 they set up the Dutch East India Company to do this. In 1619 the Dutch founded the town of Batavia in Indonesia, taking control of that country and calling it the East Indies.

TERRA AUSTRALIS Many people believed there was a large continent in the South Pacific or Indian Ocean to balance those in the northern hemisphere and prevent the world falling over. The Dutch explorer Willem Janszoon actually landed on the northeast tip of Australia in 1605–6, when some members of his crew were killed by the first Aboriginals ever seen by Europeans. Other

The Peoples of Australia and New Zealand

Australia and New Zealand were both inhabited at the time of the first European visits. In Australia, the people known as Aboriginals had probably been there for many thousands of years. They lived in different tribes, which each had its own language.

The Aboriginals were great artists and painted pictures on bark, on the ground and on the walls of caves. They led a mainly nomadic life, hunting, fishing and gathering berries.

The Maori had probably come to New Zealand from Polynesia in about AD 1350.

Maori society was very warlike and boys were taught martial arts from an early age. The Maori were also very skilled woodcarvers. The clubs that they used for fighting were very elaborate.

Below. This sixteenth-century Maori bone box was made to hold the bones of the child of a chieftain.

Above. A view of Batavia on the island of Java in what is now Indonesia. In the early seventeenth century it was the headquarters of the Dutch East India Company and a base from where the Dutch could protect their hold on the spice trade.

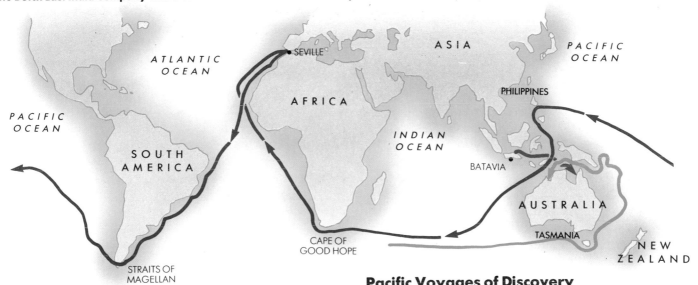

Pacific Voyages of Discovery

← Magellan's voyage   ← Janszoon's voyage

← Tasman's voyage

Dutch explorers sighted or landed at points on the northern and western coasts of Australia over the next 20 years, but the land they saw was thought to be too poor to be the continent they were looking for. They expected this new continent to contain great riches.

TASMAN'S VOYAGES In 1642 Anthony van Dieman, the governor-general of Batavia, commissioned Abel Tasman (1603–1659) to explore the South Pacific. Tasman sailed further south than Janszoon had done and saw Tasmania, which he called Van Dieman's Land, and New Zealand. His journey home took him to Tonga and Fiji. On his second voyage, in 1644, he sailed along the north coast of Australia. It was still thought to be a poor place, and no attempts at colonization were made.

Below. The Dutch sailor Abel Tasman. His voyages proved that Australia was not joined to the islands of the Dutch East Indies. However, people still believed that there was another continent to be discovered in the south.

Above. The most northerly route on this map is the one followed by Ferdinand Magellan and Juan Sebastian del Cano after they left Seville in 1519 to sail around the world. The other routes are those followed by Tasman when he set out from Batavia to explore the south Pacific.

49

TOWARDS OVERSEAS EMPIRES

An engraving of an indigo factory in the West Indies. Indigo was a plant which grew well there. It was used as a dark blue dye by the European textile industry.

At the end of the fifteenth century, Portugal and Spain were the dominant powers in Europe. They were also the most interested in sponsoring long-distance voyages to discover new routes to India and the spice-producing countries. During the sixteenth century, however, strong rulers came to power in England and in France, and the Netherlands declared its independence from Spain. This led to conflict within Europe as different rulers tried to dominate the continent. The conflict was then repeated overseas as England, France and the Netherlands joined in the search for new routes and new lands.

THE LINE OF DEMARCATION

In 1493 the pope realized that the Portuguese and Spanish voyages might lead to trouble between the two countries. To avoid this, he drew an imaginary "line of demarcation" around the world, running from north to south through a point which was 563 kilometers to the west of the Azores and the Cape Verde Islands. It touched the east coast of South America, before continuing around the world. Spain could claim land to the west of this line and Portugal could claim land to the east.

THE TREATY OF TORDESILLAS

Neither Spain nor Portugal was completely satisfied with the Line of Demarcation and so in 1494 they agreed to change it. By the Treaty of Tordesillas, the line was moved to a point 2084 kilometers west of the Cape Verde Islands. This was later to give Portugal territory in eastern Brazil, even though that country was not known to the Europeans until 1500.

THE TREATY OF SARAGOSSA

The Line of Demarcation gave Portugal the right to claim the Philippines. Spain recognized this right in the Treaty of Saragossa, which was drawn up to set a new line to the east of the Moluccas (Spice Islands). In later treaties between the two countries, Portugal gave up its claim to the Philippines in return for the whole of Brazil.

NEW CLAIMS TO TERRITORY

England, France and the Netherlands ignored the Line of Demarcation and other claims made by Spain and Portugal and started to claim land and trading rights for themselves. By 1600, all three countries had established colonies in the West Indies and in North America. The English and the French traded with India, while the Dutch controlled the East Indies.

The colony of New Amsterdam was founded by the Dutch on Manhattan Island in America in 1624. When the British captured it in 1664, the name was changed to New York.

Left. A view of Bombay harbor in India in the seventeenth century. Portugal controlled the town from 1534 to 1661. It was then given to the king of England as part of the dowry of the Portuguese princess, Catherine of Braganza, who married Charles II.

1 Throughout this period, much of Europe was troubled by war, and by outbreaks of plague and other illnesses. There were also occasional famines when the crops failed or were destroyed by armies.

2 Harvard University was founded in Cambridge, Massachusetts, in 1636. It was the first university in what is now the USA, but there was already a university in Mexico, founded in 1551.

3 In 1642 Abel Tasman became the first European to see New Zealand. It was inhabited by Maoris, who had probably migrated there from the Cook Islands around 1350. They lived mainly in the North Island in large, fortified villages of wooden houses. Most of them were farmers. Some were also woodcarvers of great skill.

NORTH AMERICA

SOUTH AMERICA

EUROPE

ASIA

AFRICA

AUSTRALIA

THE NEW BALANCE OF POWER The overseas discoveries encouraged economic growth in Europe. New markets were found, as well as new sources of raw materials such as cotton, sugar and tobacco. These were especially important to England, France and the Netherlands, all of which had growing industries.

In contrast, Portugal still relied solely on trade and Spain depended on silver from its American colonies to pay for manufactured goods from the rest of Europe. As a result, the power of Spain and Portugal gradually declined, while England, France and the Netherlands became richer and more dominant. By 1650 the balance of power within Europe had shifted towards these three countries, while the importance of their territories overseas was beginning to reflect the same distribution of power.

Above. This map shows how the European powers had begun to divide the world up between themselves by the middle of the seventeenth century. England, France and the Netherlands ignored the imaginary lines which had divided the world between Portugal and Spain. They began to set up trading links and colonies of their own. Using raw materials from the colonies to supply their growing industries at home,

- Spanish possessions
- Portuguese possessions
- British possessions
- French possessions
- Dutch possessions
- Danish possessions

England, France and the Netherlands became more important as Spain and Portugal declined.

THE OTTOMAN EMPIRE

In 1453 the Ottoman Turks, led by Mehmet II (1451–1481) captured the Byzantine capital of Constantinople and made it into the center of a Muslim empire. By 1500 this empire included the whole of Turkey, Greece and the Crimea. Although it was a Muslim empire, its rulers, or *sultans*, were tolerant of other religions, so long as their followers paid a *tribute* either in money or in men. The *Orthodox Christians* who had lived in the Byzantine Empire knew that the Catholics would never be so tolerant of them and so they paid their tribute and often fought alongside the Muslims against the Holy Roman Empire.

THE SULTAN'S PERSONAL SLAVES

To make sure that all the members of his armed forces and his government stayed faithful to him, Mehmet II decided to make them all into his personal slaves. These included many Christian youths from the Balkans who were brought to Constantinople as part of the Christian tribute and converted to Islam for a lifetime of service to the sultan. Some of them joined the Janissary corps, which was the part of the army whose job was to protect the sultan. Others were given a good education and became government officers and civil servants. After Mehmet's death in 1481 the system continued under his successors.

Left. Suleiman the Magnificent was better known in the Ottoman Empire as Suleiman the Lawgiver, because of his legal and administrative reforms.

THE EMPIRE EXPANDS

Selim I (1512–1520) started a new period of expansion. Between 1516 and 1517 he doubled the size of the territory under his control by adding Egypt, Algeria, Syria and Palestine to it.

After Selim's death, the empire passed to his son, Suleiman, and the expansion continued. Budapest fell to the Ottomans after the Battle of Mohacs in 1526, and much of Hungary was added to the empire some years later. Suleiman's army went on to capture Armenia and parts of Persia (modern-day Iraq) and Croatia. It also besieged Vienna, the capital of the Holy Roman Empire, but failed to capture the city.

THE GOLDEN AGE OF SULEIMAN

The Ottoman Empire gained great wealth through trade, because of its position at the crossroads of some of the busiest trade routes between Asia and Europe. In its markets there were goods such as woollen cloth from England, silk from Persia, *porcelain* from China and

The Ottoman Empire

CRIMEA

• BUDAPEST

BLACK SEA

GREECE • CONSTANTINOPLE

PERSIA

TURKEY

ALGERIA MEDITERRANEAN SEA SYRIA

EGYPT

RED SEA

Above. By 1645, the Ottoman Empire had expanded so far that its rulers controlled land in three continents.

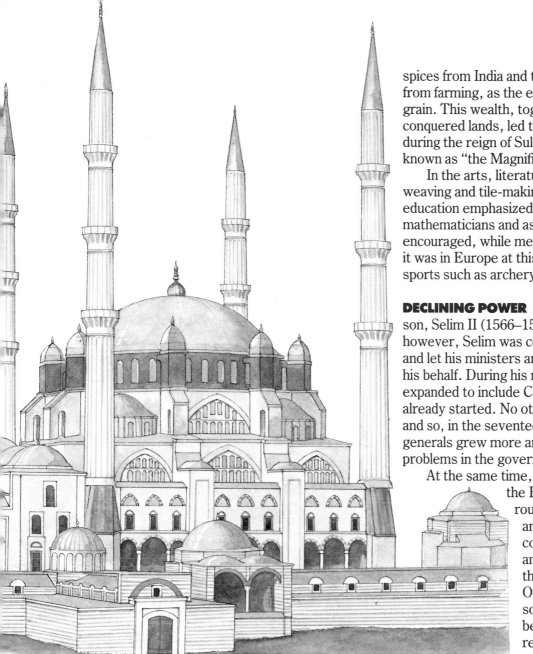

spices from India and the Far East. Wealth also came from farming, as the empire was a great producer of grain. This wealth, together with the newly conquered lands, led to a Golden Age for the empire during the reign of Suleiman I (1520–1566), who was known as "the Magnificent."

In the arts, literature, architecture, carpet-weaving and tile-making flourished. Although education emphasized religious studies, mathematicians and astronomers were also encouraged, while medicine was more advanced than it was in Europe at this time. People also enjoyed sports such as archery and wrestling.

DECLINING POWER Suleiman was succeeded by his son, Selim II (1566–1574). Unlike his father, however, Selim was content to lead a life of leisure and let his ministers and generals run the empire on his behalf. During his reign, the Ottoman Empire expanded to include Cyprus, but its decline had already started. No other sultan had Suleiman's ability and so, in the seventeenth century, the ministers and generals grew more and more powerful, which created problems in the government.

At the same time, trade became less important as the Europeans found new trade routes to India and the Far East and began to deal with these countries directly, saving time and money, instead of going through the lands of the Ottoman Empire. The great source of their wealth, trade, began to dwindle, though it remained a great center of learning.

Above. As the Islamic faith spread through the empire, Ottoman architects designed many new mosques like this one, with domed roofs and slender minarets.

Right. Selim II tried to gain control over the whole of the Mediterranean, so the Holy Roman Empire and Spain, together with some Italian states, sent a combined fleet to attack the Ottoman navy. The two sides joined battle on October 7, 1571, off the town of Lepanto in the Gulf of Corinth, Greece. The Ottoman navy was defeated and is said to have lost at least 20,000 men.

Below. Suleiman encouraged the arts and crafts in his empire. Craftsmen wove beautiful carpets from wool on handlooms and made patterned tiles to decorate the walls of houses. They also made large storage jars like this one.

THE EMERGENCE OF RUSSIA

After Constantinople was captured by the Ottoman Empire in 1453, Moscow became the new center of the Orthodox religion. Tsar Ivan III (1462–1505) married the niece of the last Byzantine emperor in 1472 and took as his emblem the Byzantine emblem of a double-headed eagle. He was responsible for the creation of a new Russian state, declaring himself independent from the *Tartars* who had been overlords of Russia for almost 250 years. Ivan III expanded his territory to include Novgorod and other cities, making Moscow his capital and rebuilding its *Kremlin*, which had been badly damaged by two fires in the 1460s.

IVAN THE TERRIBLE Ivan III was succeeded by his son, Vasili III (1505–1533), who was in turn succeeded by his three-year-old son,

Early Russia

BARENTS SEA

FINLAND

BALTIC SEA

SIBERIA

RUSSIA

• NOVGOROD
SMOLENSK • KAZAN
• MOSCOW

• KIEV

ASTRAKHAN

BLACK SEA

CASPIAN SEA

Right. St. Basil's Cathedral in Moscow was built between 1554 and 1560 after Ivan IV's victories in Kazan and Astrakhan. It was designed by two Russians called Posnik and Barma. The cathedral was originally dedicated to the Virgin Mary, but became known as St. Basil's after Basil, a Russian saint, was buried there in the reign of Ivan IV's son, Fyodor.

Above. By the end of Ivan III's reign, the territory ruled from Moscow included Pskov and Novgorod. Ivan IV wanted to expand still further to give Russia access to the Baltic Sea. This led to an unsuccessful war against Poland and Lithuania and in 1584 the port of Archangel was built on the White Sea coast instead. Towards the end of Ivan IV's reign, the territory also started to expand to the east as the exploration of Siberia began. By 1649 the Russians had access to the Pacific Ocean.

54

Ivan IV (1533–1584). This young king was crowned tsar of Russia in 1547 and by 1555 had reformed the legal system and local government. His territories increased when his armies took Kazan and Astrakhan from the Tartars, while his influence grew when he set up trading connections with England.

However, Ivan IV had had a harsh upbringing and this turned him into a brutal man. From 1560 onwards he had thousands of people executed and in 1581 he killed his eldest son in a fit of rage. This earned him the name of "Ivan the Terrible." After his death, he was succeeded by his second son, Fyodor (1584–1598).

BORIS GODUNOV AND THE TIME OF TROUBLES

Boris Godunov (1598–1605) rose to power in the reign of Ivan IV. He was regent for Fyodor until the latter died in 1598. As Fyodor had no children and his younger brother Dmitri had died before him, Boris Godunov was elected tsar.

The Time of Troubles began after Boris Godunov's death, when the so-called False Dmitri claimed the throne, saying that he was the son of Ivan IV. He was backed by Poland. He was killed in 1606, but a second False Dmitri claimed the throne two years later. This claimant was murdered in 1610, but a third False Dmitri appeared between 1611 and 1612. The Time of Troubles finally ended when Michael Romanov was elected tsar in 1613.

THE FIRST ROMANOV

Michael Romanov (1613–1645) was a weak ruler and relied heavily on his father, who was the head of the Russian Church. In spite of this weakness, Michael ruled Russia for 32 years and started a *dynasty* which lasted for 300 years. *Serfdom* increased during his reign and the Cossacks began to lose some of their independence.

THE COSSACKS

The Cossacks were descended from the Tartars and from escaped serfs. They were expert horsemen and lived in independent communities in southwest Russia. They received special privileges from the Russian rulers in exchange for military sevice.

THE SETTLEMENT OF SIBERIA

A Cossack called Yermak captured the town of Sibir from the Tartars in 1581. This victory gave the name Siberia to the whole region between the Ural Mountains and the Pacific. Other Russians followed and by 1600 they had founded a settlement at Tobolsk. They then traveled east along the great rivers, defeating the native tribes as they went.

In 1649 the Russians reached the Pacific, then turned south to Lake Baikal, founding the town of Irkutsk in 1651. The fur trade made Siberia important and the defeated tribes had to pay a tribute in furs to the Russian government. Once Siberia had been opened up, many peasants went there to escape from serfdom.

Above. This picture shows Russians travelling in sledges known as troikas. They used these sleds to travel long distances.

Right. Ivan the Terrible was an intelligent man who wrote well and composed prayers and music for the Church. He encouraged art and literature and the use of printing in his country. He married six times; three wives died, two were divorced and one outlived him.

Russian Peasantry

The peasants in Russia lived as serfs, or slaves, on the estates of wealthy noblemen. They had no rights and few possessions. Their homes were often flimsy and gave little protection against the icy cold winters. In times of famine many of them died of illnesses brought on by hunger. This was especially true when the crops failed between 1601 and 1603. Thousands died, while others turned to robbery and cannibalism in order to survive.

In the unrest after the death of Boris Godunov, however, many serfs escaped to make new lives for themselves in Siberia.

THE MOGUL EMPIRE OF INDIA

At the end of the fifteenth century, Babur (1495–1530), a descendant of the Mongol leader Genghis Khan, became the ruler of Fergana in Turkestan. He hoped to reconquer his ancestors' kingdom of Samarkand, but failed, turning his attention instead to Afghanistan and capturing Kabul. From there he raided India and in 1526 he led his troops down the Khyber Pass and onto the plains of India. He defeated and killed the sultan of Delhi in battle, and the following year he defeated the Rajputs in a battle near Agra. Although the Rajputs were the best soldiers in India, Babur was able to defeat them as they rode into battle on elephants, while his men were mounted on swift-moving horses. After this victory, he soon took control of the whole of northern India and became the first ruler of an empire which was to last, in some form, until 1857.

THE EARLY YEARS OF THE MOGUL DYNASTY The
empire which Babur founded was known as the Mogul Empire. Its survival in the early years was uncertain, for when Babur died, his son, Humayun (1530–1556), was at first unable to hold the throne. After 10 years of fighting, Humayan was driven out of India and into Persia (Iraq).

Above. The Taj Mahal at Agra is probably the most famous building in India. It was built for Mumtaz-i-Mahal, wife of the Mogul Emperor Shah Jahan, and they are both buried here. It took more than 20,000 workmen 22 years to construct the building, which is made of pure white marble, inlaid with precious stones. Shah Jahan was the grandson of Akbar but, unlike his grandfather, he was a ruthless ruler.

Mogul India

Above. The Mogul Empire. It was founded by Babur, who began by raiding India from his base in Afghanistan and later took control of the north of the country. By the time Babur's grandson, Akbar, became emperor, the empire stretched as far south as central India.

Below. Emperor Jahangir (1605–1627) looking at a portrait of his father, Akbar. Jahangir was a wise and just ruler who expanded the Mogul Empire and encouraged sports and the arts. He also encouraged trade with Britain through the East India Company.

Above. Part of the city of Fatehpur Sikri in Uttar Pradesh in northern India. It was built for Emperor Akbar in a mixture of Hindu and Muslim styles of architecture. It is now deserted, but from 1569 to 1585 it was the capital of the Mogul Empire.

Right. As these dagger handles show, craftsmen of the Mogul Empire were skilled at working with jade, gold and precious stones. Others painted pictures, especially miniatures showing scenes from court life, legends and history.

In 1555 he started to reconquer his empire, but before he achieved very much he died in an accident, leaving his 14-year-old son Akbar to fight for the throne.

REGAINING THE EMPIRE When Akbar (1556–1605) came to the throne of Hindustan, the whole of India was in a state of civil war as Hindus and Muslims struggled for power. Because Akbar was so young, his mother and her courtiers ruled for him for four years, then he determined to rule for himself and started out to recover the territory that had been lost. By the time of his death he had achieved this and more, leaving an empire which stretched from the Hindu Kush Mountains in the north to the Godavari River in central India.

THE WISDOM OF AKBAR Because Akbar realized that there would be no peace in his empire while there were differences between the Muslims and the Hindus, he decided to treat both religions equally. Although he was a Muslim himself, he married a Hindu princess. Akbar was also prepared to listen to the beliefs of others and allowed the Jesuit missionaries into India. He set up a system of law which gave Muslims and Hindus the right to be tried

according to their own customs. He also changed the method of tax collection, so that the peasants knew in advance how much they ought to pay and were therefore less likely to be robbed by dishonest tax collectors.

Although Akbar could neither read nor write, he encouraged literature and painting, as well as architecture, and he held a brilliant court in his capital city of Agra. He also had a city at Fatehpur Sikri built for him in a combination of Muslim and Hindu styles of architecture.

THE FIRST EUROPEANS IN INDIA India was a land with many riches. It produced gold and jewels, as well as beautifully printed cloths like cottons and muslins. It also grew many of the spices which the Europeans wanted, including pepper, cinnamon and ginger.

The Portuguese were the first Europeans to come to India in search of these products, but they were soon followed by the English and the Dutch, all of whom set up trading colonies. In 1600 the British East India Company was founded and, as the power of the Mogul emperors began to wane in the early eighteenth century, this company started to affect every aspect of life in India.

THE MING DYNASTY OF CHINA

Left. Chinese landscape artists painted what they thought was important, instead of exact copies of real scenes.

China under the Ming Dynasty

Above. The Chinese empire during the Ming Dynasty. It was cut off by high mountains, deserts and oceans. Its emperors distrusted foreigners. Traders found it very difficult to do business in China at this time.

The Ming Dynasty was at the height of its power in the sixteenth century. It was founded in 1368 by Chu Yuan-chang, who freed his country from the control of the *Mongols*. He and his successors brought a period of stability and prosperity to their country, but, in reaction to the period of Mongol rule, the Ming emperors looked down on anything that was foreign. Because of this, the European traders who visited China in the sixteenth century were treated as inferiors and their activities were compared to piracy.

The missionaries who followed the traders did not fare much better, as the Chinese already had well-established religions of their own. Some people were Taoists and some were Buddhists, but the majority followed the teachings of Confucius.

CONFUCIUS Confucius (*c.* 551–478 BC) was a Chinese philosopher who believed that people were born good and that they had a moral duty to each other. He thought sincerity, fearlessness, wisdom and compassion were important. He also thought that people should know their place in society and be content with it. Confucius made strict rules about this.

Everyone, from the poorest peasant to the emperor himself, was expected to conform to these rules and to live in harmony with nature. These ideas were known as Confucianism and belief in them helped the Ming emperors to be successful.

CHINESE SOCIETY The Confucianist ideal was a mainly agricultural population living under an educated *bureaucracy* which in turn was guided by a wise and compassionate emperor. For two centuries the Ming Dynasty managed to achieve this ideal.
The government

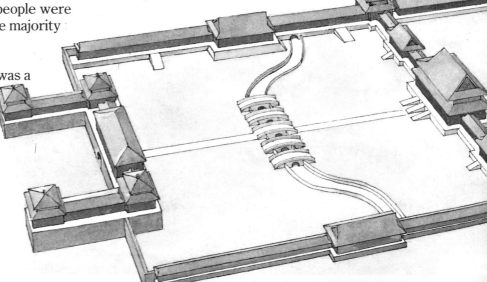

encouraged irrigation schemes which allowed the rice to be harvested twice a year. It also encouraged the growth of cash crops such as cotton and tea. It paved roads, built bridges, and enlarged the canal system to avoid a long stretch of dangerous coastline.

These schemes and many others were paid for by taxes which were collected by many hundreds of government officials, called mandarins. These men reached their positions by passing examinations and not by inheriting them from their fathers.

ARTS AND CRAFTS IN MING CHINA This period of peace and prosperity led to a flowering of arts and crafts in China. Encouraged by the emperors, some artists made beautifully painted and glazed porcelain. Others wove silk brocades or produced elaborate *lacquerwork* boxes and screens. Printing reached high standards and many people painted pictures. At first these were mainly of birds and flowers, but later landscape painting also became popular.

THE COLLAPSE OF THE MING DYNASTY Early in the seventeenth century, the Ming Dynasty began to weaken. Sending the Ming armies to defeat the Japanese in Korea in 1592 and 1597 proved very costly and after this came a peasant rising in western China and a famine in the north. In Beijing (Peking) officials struggled with each other to gain power, and also raised taxes while leaving the army unpaid. At the same time, the emperors became mainly interested in their own power and wealth.

THE RISE OF THE MANCHUS As the Ming Dynasty declined, the tribes of Manchuria in northeast China united under a chief called Nurhachi. In 1618 the Manchus over-ran the Ming province of Liaotung. Nurhachi died in 1626, but his successors soon took control of northern China and set up a new dynasty.

Chinese Dress

During the Ming Dynasty, the clothes that people wore reflected their place in society. There were strict rules about every item, from the hat to the shoes.

For example, only the most important government officials could wear crimson silk robes decorated with dragons. Less important officials wore robes decorated with birds or with animals, depending on whether they worked with civilians or the army. The position of the decorations also showed the wearer's importance.

1 The Spanish capture the Philippines to increase their share of the spice market.

2 The Pilgrim Fathers set sail in 1620 to start a new life, as the Ming dynasty comes to an end.

3 Portuguese sailors visit Japan. They are the first Europeans to arrive. They eventually start a colony in Nagasaki.

Above. A high-ranking Chinese official. His silk gown was embroidered with silk threads. This, together with his very long fingernails, shows he did not have to do any manual work.

A reconstruction of the Forbidden City of Peking (Beijing) in the Ming Dynasty. Peking, the capital of Ming China, was made up of two walled cities. The Inner City, which had been the capital of Mongol China, was surrounded by a stone wall 50 feet high, 60 feet thick and 4.2 miles long on each side. To the south was the Outer City, with walls 4 miles long. Within the Inner City was the Imperial City, surrounded by red walls. The Forbidden City got its name because everyone except the emperor, his family and his closest advisers was forbidden to go in.

JAPAN AND THE SHOGUNS

At the beginning of the sixteenth century Japan was a feudal state, ruled by an emperor. Each feudal lord had his own private army of warriors known as *samurai*, and these armies were often involved in local wars against each other.

The economy of the country was based on agriculture and rice was the most important crop. Improvements in irrigation meant that it could be harvested twice a year. There was also some mining for copper and silver, but craftsmen and workers in industry were thought to have a lowly status when compared with other groups of people such as farmers and military men. Japan's nearest neighbor was China and trade between the two countries was encouraged.

Japan and its Neighbors

Right. This castle, or temple, shows the strong Chinese influence on Japanese architecture. It seems more solidly built than many in China, but it is made largely of wood and its many tiled roofs with dragon decorations are very much like those on Chinese buildings from the same period. The colors are also similar to the ones that were used in China.

Left. Japan is a series of islands, separated from the mainland of Asia by the sea. For centuries the Chinese were the only people from outside to visit Japan. They set up trading links and had a great influence on Japanese architecture and religion. The first Europeans reached Japan in 1543. They were welcomed at first, but in less than a century Japan had isolated itself from the rest of the world once more and nearly all links with foreigners were cut.

THE EMPEROR AND THE SHOGUN   Legend has it that the first emperor of Japan was Jimmu, who ruled in around 660 BC, and that all the emperors who followed were descended from him. At first the country was ruled by powerful emperors. However, from the twelfth century onwards the emperors became sacred, shadowy figures, often living in monasteries, and the real power was in the hands of a nobleman known as the shogun.

THE FIRST EUROPEANS   In 1543 a party of Portuguese sailors became the first people from Europe to visit Japan. Six years later Francis Xavier, a Spanish priest, arrived and began to convert some of the Japanese to Roman Catholicism. This encouraged more missionaries to come from Spain and Portugal and traders came with them. At the start of the seventeenth century, other traders came from England and from the Netherlands.

HIDEYOSHI AS SHOGUN   In 1585 Hideyoshi became the shogun. He was a great warrior and planned to build a large Japanese empire which would include China. In 1592 and 1597 his armies got as far as Korea, but both times they failed to conquer it.

THE TOKUGAWA SHOGUNATE   In 1603 Ieyasu became the shogun. He was from the Tokugawa family, which

was to rule Japan for the next 250 years. Ieyasu was a wise statesman who had been Hideyoshi's chief deputy in eastern Japan. Under his rule, the warfare between the local samurai bands was brought to an end and a time of peace and prosperity began. He achieved this by dividing the country into about 250 regions called domains. Each domain was led by a *daimyo*, who controlled the samurai and had to swear allegiance to the Tokugawa shogunate.

KEEPING LAW AND ORDER   During the early years of the Tokugawa shogunate, Japan became isolated from the rest of the world once more. Ieyasu was afraid that the missionaries from Europe might bring armies with them to conquer Japan, and so he and the shoguns who followed him decided to rid Japan of Christianity. The missionaries had to leave and the Japanese converts had to give up their religion or be killed.

The Tokugawa shoguns also thought that the only way to keep law and order within Japan was by ending contact with the rest of the world. In the 1630s almost all ties with other nations were cut. Only the Dutch were allowed to keep one small trading station in the harbor at Nagasaki. All other foreigners had to leave and Japanese people who were abroad at the time were not allowed to return home. By 1650 Japan's isolation was complete.

Ieyasu's Capital at Edo

Towards the end of the sixteenth century, Edo was a small fishing village of about 100 houses built around a castle. Then in 1590 Hideyoshi gave the castle to Tokugawa Ieyusa, along with a large amount of land in the area.

Ieyasu made Edo into his principal castle and, when he became shogun, Edo

became his administrative centre. He had land reclaimed from the sea, drained marshes and diverted the river to make room for the new city which spread out like a spider's web around the castle.

About 80,000 samurai moved to Edo and all the daimyos had to have a house there and spend some of their time in it. By

Above. Tokugawa Ieyasu, who founded the Tokugawa shogunate. He kept a strict control over all the other noble families in Japan. He also encouraged agriculture and Confucianism.

1613 the population was estimated to be 150,000. It included craftsmen, merchants and commoners.

Left. Japanese society at this time was very strict and rigid. Manners and etiquette were very formal and it was thought better to be dead than to lose respect or honor. Within society, military men were the most important group, followed by farmers, then craftsmen and industrial workers. Women were treated almost as decorations. As you can see from this picture, their clothes were very impractical. Their wide sleeves made it almost impossible for them to do any work, while their flowing gowns and high shoes made it hard for them to walk. All the pins and combs in their hair made it difficult for women even to move their heads.

Africa and the Americas
THE EMPIRES OF AFRICA

The continent of Africa at this time was made up of many different peoples, cultures, kingdoms and empires. Many of the empires were based on long-distance trading across the deserts and grasslands. The goods which were traded included gold, salt and ivory. People captured in war or by raiding parties in the south were sold as slaves in the north, while others were sold as slaves to India and Arabia. Those empires which touched the coasts of Africa became known to European traders during this period. The Europeans were not interested in the interior of Africa, however, and most of it remained a mystery to them until they explored it in the nineteenth century.

THE ISLAMIC INFLUENCE The north and east of Africa had been under Islamic influence from the late seventh century AD. The Friday Mosque at Kairouan in Tunisia was founded in 670 and Islam spread west from there through Algeria and into Morocco. The religion also spread south across the Sahara Desert and reached trading centers such as Timbuktu, Gao and Jenne by the eleventh century. Islam was also important along the east coast of Africa, which was nearest to Arabia. The adoption of the Islamic religion and way of life brought a long period of stability to many parts of Africa. It also encouraged trade between Africa and the rest of the Islamic world.

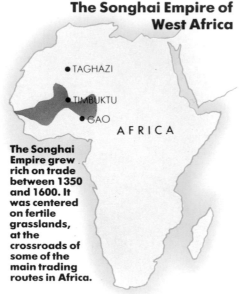

The Songhai Empire of West Africa

- TAGHAZI
- TIMBUKTU
- GAO

AFRICA

The Songhai Empire grew rich on trade between 1350 and 1600. It was centered on fertile grasslands, at the crossroads of some of the main trading routes in Africa.

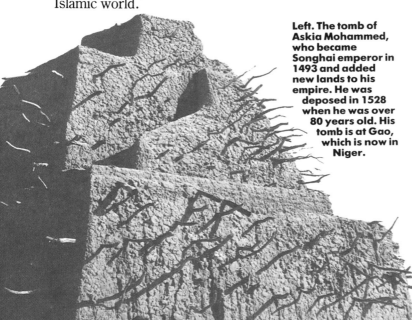

Left. The tomb of Askia Mohammed, who became Songhai emperor in 1493 and added new lands to his empire. He was deposed in 1528 when he was over 80 years old. His tomb is at Gao, which is now in Niger.

THE SUDANESE EMPIRES The vast grasslands of Africa which lay to the south of the Sahara Desert were known as the Sudan. From medieval times they were dominated by a series of empires whose wealth was built up on trade.

Between about 1350 and 1600 the most important of these was the Songhai Empire, which stretched from the coast of West Africa to the shores of Lake Chad. Its two main trading centers were the cities of Gao and Timbuktu, where gold from the forest lands to the south was exchanged for salt from Taghazi in the desert to the north. Cotton goods, copper, slaves and even dried seafish were also traded. The goods were carried on horseback or camel, depending on whether they were crossing the grasslands or the desert. The Songhai Empire started to collapse in 1591 when it was invaded by Moroccans from the north.

THE EAST COAST Many ports and city-states on the east coast of Africa had grown important through trade. As they were on the Indian Ocean they had links with Arabia, India and even China. Their main exports were metals (including gold, copper and iron), ivory, tortoiseshell and a small number of slaves. These were exchanged for cotton and beads from India, luxury items such as silks and brocades, and porcelain from China. From 1500 onwards, these cities were taken over by Portuguese traders and the pattern of trade was changed.

THE SLAVE TRADE There had always been a slave trade in Africa, but until the sixteenth century it had been on a very small scale. After the Europeans began to settle in the Americas in the sixteenth century, that started to change. The Europeans found the climate of the Americas too hot for them to work in and so they enslaved the native Indians to do the work for them. Then, as a mixture of ill-treatment and disease killed most of the Indians, increasing numbers of Africans were transported to the Americas to take their places in the mines and on the plantations.

Above. Timbuktu, a major city in the Songhai Empire. In the early sixteenth century it was described as a city of learning. The king was said to have an army of 3000 cavalry. The city had many magistrates, learned doctors and religious men, as well as a big market for the sale of books. It was a center of Islamic culture and its mosque is now the oldest in West Africa. Its wealth was built on trade, but it started to decline after it was invaded by the Moroccans in 1591.

Below. The ruins of one of the castles built by King Fasilidas at Gondar in Ethiopia. He ruled from 1632 to 1665 and Gondar was his capital.

1 In 1497 John Cabot discovered Newfoundland. He was probably the first European to go there since the Vikings.

2 Between 1554 and 1556 the Ottoman Turks expanded their empire by conquering the coast of North Africa.

3 Until the 1580s the calendar used in Europe was the Julian calendar, introduced by Julius Caesar in 46 BC. This was based on a year which was 11 minutes and 14 seconds longer than the time the earth actually takes to orbit the sun, so by the 1580s the calendar was wrong by 10 days. Pope Gregory corrected this in 1582 by making 5 October into 15 October. Roman Catholic countries adopted this Gregorian calendar straight away. Many Protestant countries did not change until 1700, and Britain waited until 1752.

Arts and Crafts of the Songhai Empire

The people of the Songhai Empire were skilled metal-workers. Gold and copper were brought to the trading centers of Gao and Timbuktu. Here the craftsmen mixed copper with tin to make bronze, which they made into intricately patterned bowls and cups, jewelry and ornaments. Sometimes they added a thin layer of gold, called gilt.

Some potters produced realistic human statues and heads, others made patterned tiles for decoration. Other craft-workers included cotton weavers who made fine cloth for export.

Woodcarvings from the Songhai Empire. Some carvers made realistic statues like the one in the middle. Others carved shapes which followed the natural lines of the wood they were using.

63

CENTRAL AND SOUTH AMERICAN EMPIRES

This Aztec knife was probably used at special ceremonies. It has a stone blade because the Aztecs did not know how to make metal into tools.

Prior to European landings in the "new world" in the sixteenth century, several highly developed societies thrived in the swamps, jungles and mountains of Central and South America. Perhaps the most highly developed of all early American societies, however, were the Aztecs of Central America and the Incas of the high Andes Mountains in modern-day Peru.

THE AZTECS The people known as Aztecs arrived in Mexico in the twelfth century, and settled on an island in Lake Texcoco. By the fourteenth century, through a process of land reclamation, they had made their island much bigger and had built a flourishing city there called Tenochtitlan. In the early sixteenth century there were probably around 150,000 people living there.

Aztec society was highly militaristic. A large, well-equipped professional army was maintained which was dedicated to conquering new territory and acquiring *tribute*. Gold, cotton, turquoise, feathers, food and a whole host of other commodities were sent as tribute to Tenochtitlan. These were all itemized on detailed tribute lists, many of which still survive.

HUMAN SACRIFICES The most significant of all tributes was a huge number of human beings, all of whom were destined for sacrifice in Tenochtitlan. The Aztecs believed that the offering of human sacrifices was the only way to please their sun god, Huitzilopochtli. Most sacrifices involved cutting out the heart of the victim whilst he or she was stretched out on a stone slab before the temple of the god. The scale of human sacrifice was enormous. At the consecration of a new temple in Tenochtitlan in 1487, as many as 20,000 men and women were ritually murdered over four days.

Left. Humans being sacrificed at Tenochtitlan. The priest killed them in a way that made their hearts spring out as he cut them.

Above. The Aztecs valued the feathers of brightly colored birds and accepted them as tribute from people they had conquered. The feathers were used to decorate objects such as this ceremonial shield.

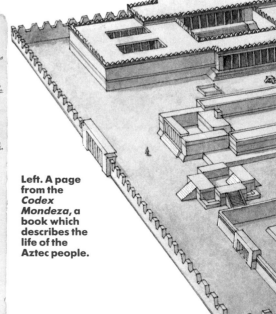

Left. A page from the *Codex Mondeza*, a book which describes the life of the Aztec people.

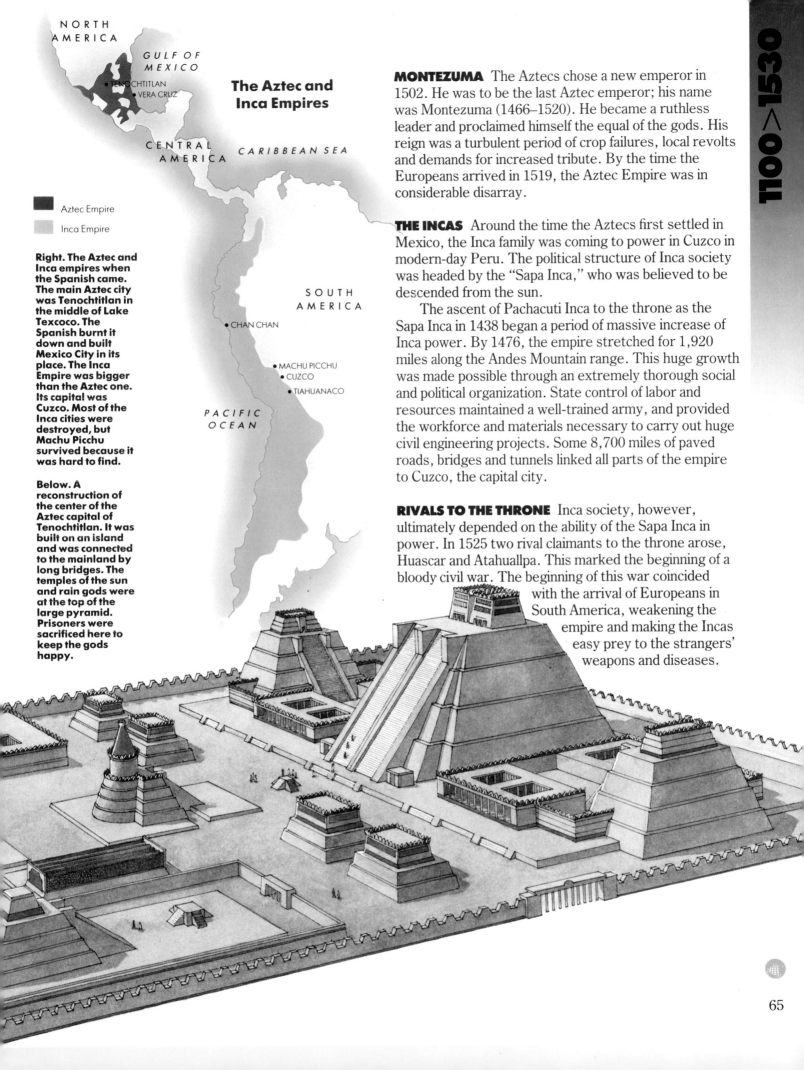

The Aztec and Inca Empires

NORTH AMERICA

GULF OF MEXICO

• TENOCHTITLAN
• VERA CRUZ

CENTRAL AMERICA

CARIBBEAN SEA

SOUTH AMERICA

• CHAN CHAN

• MACHU PICCHU
• CUZCO
• TIAHUANACO

PACIFIC OCEAN

■ Aztec Empire
□ Inca Empire

Right. The Aztec and Inca empires when the Spanish came. The main Aztec city was Tenochtitlan in the middle of Lake Texcoco. The Spanish burnt it down and built Mexico City in its place. The Inca Empire was bigger than the Aztec one. Its capital was Cuzco. Most of the Inca cities were destroyed, but Machu Picchu survived because it was hard to find.

Below. A reconstruction of the center of the Aztec capital of Tenochtitlan. It was built on an island and was connected to the mainland by long bridges. The temples of the sun and rain gods were at the top of the large pyramid. Prisoners were sacrificed here to keep the gods happy.

MONTEZUMA The Aztecs chose a new emperor in 1502. He was to be the last Aztec emperor; his name was Montezuma (1466–1520). He became a ruthless leader and proclaimed himself the equal of the gods. His reign was a turbulent period of crop failures, local revolts and demands for increased tribute. By the time the Europeans arrived in 1519, the Aztec Empire was in considerable disarray.

THE INCAS Around the time the Aztecs first settled in Mexico, the Inca family was coming to power in Cuzco in modern-day Peru. The political structure of Inca society was headed by the "Sapa Inca," who was believed to be descended from the sun.

The ascent of Pachacuti Inca to the throne as the Sapa Inca in 1438 began a period of massive increase of Inca power. By 1476, the empire stretched for 1,920 miles along the Andes Mountain range. This huge growth was made possible through an extremely thorough social and political organization. State control of labor and resources maintained a well-trained army, and provided the workforce and materials necessary to carry out huge civil engineering projects. Some 8,700 miles of paved roads, bridges and tunnels linked all parts of the empire to Cuzco, the capital city.

RIVALS TO THE THRONE Inca society, however, ultimately depended on the ability of the Sapa Inca in power. In 1525 two rival claimants to the throne arose, Huascar and Atahuallpa. This marked the beginning of a bloody civil war. The beginning of this war coincided with the arrival of Europeans in South America, weakening the empire and making the Incas easy prey to the strangers' weapons and diseases.

AMERICA: CONTACTS WITH SPAIN AND PORTUGAL

By the end of the fifteenth century the monarchs of both Portugal and Spain wanted to expand their territories and gain new wealth for themselves and their countries. They hoped to do this by opening up new trade routes to the east, but instead they came across America. After conquering the islands of the West Indies, they sent expeditions to the mainland, going first to Mexico, then to South America and finally to California, Arizona and New Mexico.

CORTES AND THE AZTECS Hernando Cortes (1485–1547) was born in Spain and went to Hispaniola in the West Indies when he was a young man. From there he took part in the conquest of Cuba and in 1518 was chosen to lead an expedition to Mexico with about 500 Spanish soldiers and about 300 Indians who had become their allies. He also took firearms and cannons, as well as mastiff dogs and 16 horses, none of which the Aztecs had ever seen before.

When Cortes arrived at Tenochtitlan, the Aztec Emperor Montezuma (see p. 64) thought he was the god Quetzalcoatl and did not resist when Cortes captured him and started to rule in his place. When Cortes returned to the coast, however, the Aztecs rebelled and he went back with his army to try to put the rebellion down.

Montezuma was killed in the fighting and Cortes retreated to the coast again.

The following year Cortes returned once more to Tenochtitlan and this time destroyed it and perhaps 100,000 of its people. The rest were made into slaves. Spanish settlers took the land, and all the Aztec treasures were melted down into gold ingots and shipped back to Spain.

THE FOUNDATION OF NEW SPAIN As well as the Aztec Empire, the Spanish also conquered the territory which had belonged to the Maya and the Toltecs. In 1535 all this land became the Vice-Royalty of New Spain, governed by Antonio de Mendoza, who encouraged economic development of the area and set up the first printing press in the New World. California, Arizona and New Mexico were added to New Spain later.

PIZARRO AND THE INCAS Like Cortes, Francisco Pizarro (c. 1478–1541) was born in Spain but went to America as a young man. In 1513 he accompanied Balboa on an expedition across Panama to the Pacific and later settled there. In partnership with a soldier called Almagro, he went exploring the west coast of South America. On their travels, they heard of the rich Inca

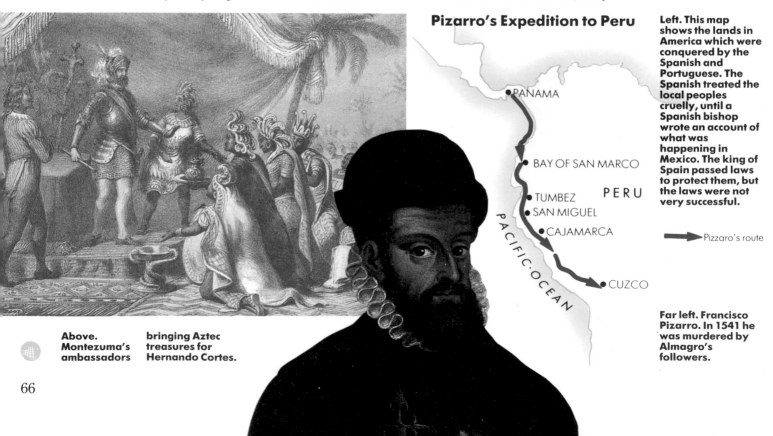

Above. Montezuma's ambassadors bringing Aztec treasures for Hernando Cortes.

Pizarro's Expedition to Peru

PANAMA

BAY OF SAN MARCO

TUMBEZ
SAN MIGUEL

PERU

CAJAMARCA

PACIFIC OCEAN

CUZCO

Pizarro's route

Left. This map shows the lands in America which were conquered by the Spanish and Portuguese. The Spanish treated the local peoples cruelly, until a Spanish bishop wrote an account of what was happening in Mexico. The king of Spain passed laws to protect them, but the laws were not very successful.

Far left. Francisco Pizarro. In 1541 he was murdered by Almagro's followers.

The Legend of El Dorado

The Spanish conquistadores spent a lot of time looking for the legendary kingdom of El Dorado, or the Golden Man, which they thought was full of gold.

The legend probably came from the Muisca people in the northern Andes. When a new king came to the throne there, he made an offering to the gods at Lake Guatavita. His body was covered with gold dust and he and his courtiers went at night to the middle of the lake on a raft. The courtiers threw gold objects into the lake and the king dived in after them. As he did so, the gold dust washed from his body and sank into the water.

By the time the Spaniards heard the legend, the Muisca had already been defeated. Their gold had been melted down and sent to Spain.

Few gold treasures survive from before the Spanish conquest of Central and South America. The Inca mask above probably represents the sun. The *tunjo* (raft) on the left was made by the Muisca and represents the raft from the El Dorado ceremony. The gold puma on the right is from the Mochica period in Peru, between the fourth and the ninth centuries AD. The puma has a human face decorating its tongue and double-headed serpents on its body.

Empire and in 1528 Pizarro returned to Spain to obtain permission to conquer the empire and become its governor. He set out in 1530 and after two unsuccessful attempts landed on the coast of Peru.

Pizarro found the empire in the midst of a civil war between Huascar, the rightful Sapa Inca, and Atahuallpa, his half-brother (see p. 65). The Europeans took advantage of the situation and, after Atahuallpa had Huascar killed, the Spanish executed Atahuallpa and set up the young Manco as ruler, although the Spanish had the real power. Pizarro and his men then seized the lands of the Incas, stole their treasures and forced the Indians into slavery.

THE PORTUGUESE IN BRAZIL Portuguese explorers landed on the coast of what is now Brazil in 1500, while they were looking for a new route to India. They claimed the land for Portugal, but at first very little was done about it as the country was not thought to have many resources other than some dye-woods. After a revolt of slaves on the African island of São Tomé in the 1570s,

The silver mines at Potosi, Bolivia, where the Spaniards used local people as slaves to remove over 18,000 tons of silver ore. The mines were worked out in the seventeenth century.

however, the Portuguese decided to move their sugar plantations from there to Brazil. This encouraged the slave trade and also made Brazil suddenly seem attractive to other European powers.

AMERICA: THE PILGRIM FATHERS

While the Spanish and Portuguese journeyed to Central and South America, and to the southern part of North America, other Europeans started to explore the northeast coast. Most of them were looking for a possible northwest passage to Asia, and it was only when they failed to find one that they started thinking about colonization.

THE FOUNDATION OF VIRGINIA In 1583 Humphrey Gilbert claimed Newfoundland for England. When he was drowned in a storm, his half-brother, Sir Walter Raleigh (1552–1618), took up his idea of setting up colonies in America. He thought this would help to solve the problems of over-population and unemployment in England and also encourage trade between the two countries. Between 1584 and 1589, Raleigh sent out six expeditions to start a colony in a place he called Virginia at the suggestion of Queen Elizabeth I. These all failed, but in 1607 the Virginia Company was set up and the first successful colony was established at Jamestown. The company hoped to make quick profits through the discovery of gold mines, or from producing wine and silk. In this they were unsuccessful, but in 1612 one of the settlers started to grow tobacco and this led to prosperity for the colony.

THE ARRIVAL OF THE PILGRIM FATHERS The Pilgrim Fathers is the name given to the group of 102 Puritans who left England on the *Mayflower* in September 1620.

Early Settlement in North America

The first European colonies in north-east America were along the coast. Some settlers went there to make money, but many went because they were persecuted for their religious beliefs at home. These groups included Roman Catholics, as well as very strict Puritans like the Pilgrim Fathers. Many Puritans were very intolerant of people who did not share their beliefs. This led to people with less strict views setting up separate colonies.

They planned to go to Virginia, but their ship took them further north and they landed at Cape Cod in November. They decided to stay in that area and searched for a site to settle in. On 11 December they arrived at Plymouth, where they built huts and a meeting house. They elected John Carver as their first governor and befriended the local Indians.

During that first winter, however, nearly half the colony died as a result of the severe weather and a lack of

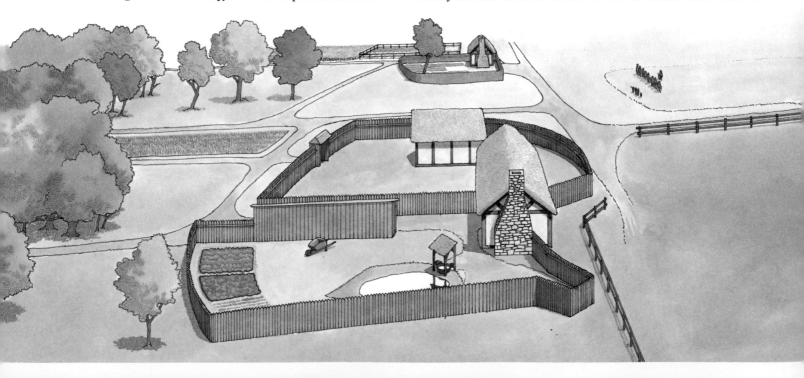

food. The rest were only saved when the ship *Fortune* arrived with food and other necessities. The *Fortune* also brought more settlers and so the colony managed to survive.

EXPANSION Once the Pilgrim Fathers were settled in Plymouth, other Puritans decided to follow them. They were given a grant of land and formed themselves into the Massachusetts Bay Company. The first group left England in 1630 and by 1640 there were over 14,000 Puritans in Massachusetts. They were intolerant of non-Puritans, however, and this led to the founding of more liberal colonies such as Rhode Island.

Meanwhile, Lord Baltimore, a Catholic, was also granted some land, which he called Maryland, in North America. He encouraged his fellow Catholics to move there. Although they were few in number, they enjoyed the equal rights and religious freedom which they had been denied in England.

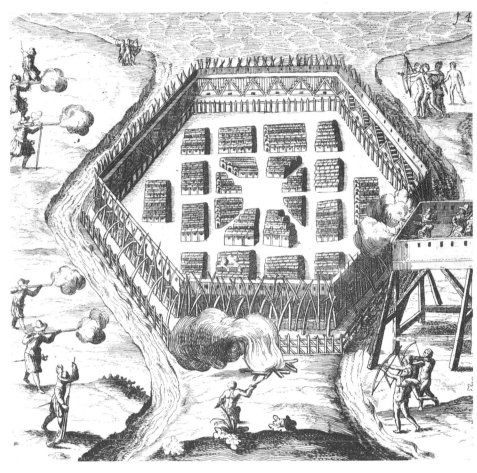

Above. Onandago Fort was set up in Quebec by Samuel de Champlain.

THE FRENCH SETTLEMENT IN CANADA A French navigator called Jacques Cartier (1494–1557) made three voyages to Canada between 1534 and 1541. On his second journey, he sailed up the St. Lawrence River with the help of two Indians, while on the third he set out to look for a mythical place called Saguenay. This expedition was a failure, but it gave France a claim to land in Canada.

Little was done about this claim until 1608, when the explorer Samuel de Champlain (1567–1635) founded the town that was to become the city of Quebec and started to organize the fur trade between France and Canada. He also formed an alliance between France and the Huron and Algonquin Indians against the Iroquois Indians. Very few French people were tempted to go to Canada at this time and the number of European settlers in this area remained small until after 1650.

A reconstruction of one of the early colonies. When the settlers landed on the coast, they looked for a site with a good supply of fresh water. Then they cleared the land by cutting down the trees, to give them firewood and building material for their houses, barns and fences. The fences protected the houses and gardens from wild animals. Each settlement usually had a large building to use as a meeting house and center for the community. This was often built inside a high fence, or stockade, to protect it against Indian attacks.

THE WEST INDIES

The West Indies in 1650

BAHAMAS

CUBA

HISPANIOLA

JAMAICA

ST KITTS
NEVIS
MONTSERRAT
GUADALOUPE
ANTIGUA

CARIBBEAN SEA

MARTINIQUE
ST LUCIA
BARBADOS

GRANADA

TRINIDAD

SOUTH AMERICA

Spanish
British
French

Above. The West Indies is a series of islands which stretches for over 2400 kilometers, from Florida to Venezuela. Most of the islands are of **volcanic origin, but some are made largely of coral. The Spanish were the first to set up colonies there, followed by the English and French.** **Right. An Arawak zemi, carved from wood, representing one of the spirits which were worshipped by the Arawaks before the Europeans arrived.**

On October 12, 1492 Christopher Columbus sighted what came to be known as the New World. He thought it was Asia, but instead it was an island in the Bahamas which he named San Salvador. He claimed it for Spain and went on to visit Cuba and Hispaniola. On later journeys he and his crew became the first Europeans to sight Jamaica, Trinidad, Honduras and Costa Rica and, although these places were inhabited by people he called Indians, Columbus claimed them all for Spain.

THE ARAWAK INDIANS The first Indians Columbus saw when he arrived in the West Indies were the Arawaks. They were farmers whose main crops were maize (corn), cotton and root crops called yams and manioc. They also grew tobacco. The Arawaks lived in large villages of as many as 3000 people in 1000 houses. According to the Spanish, their society was divided into noblemen, commoners and slaves. Their religion was based on the worship of a number of spirits

called "zemis" and they made figures of these out of stone, wood and clay. Each person owned at least one zemi, which was kept in the house and had to be offered food.

The Arawaks were a peace-loving people. They had gone to live in the Greater Antilles when the Carib Indians had migrated from the mainland and driven them from their homes in the Lesser Antilles not long before the arrival of the Spanish.

THE CARIB INDIANS In contrast to the Arawaks, the Carib Indians' chief interest was war. They were expert navigators and went raiding over long distances in large, dug-out canoes. When they captured other people, they killed the men and ate their flesh, but kept the women as slave-wives. On the islands they lived in small, independent villages, but had no leaders except in times of war. They lived by growing plants such as manioc and by hunting a range of animals for food. The weapons that the Carib used included javelins, clubs and arrows tipped with poison.

THE SPANISH SETTLERS The first Europeans to colonize the West Indies were the Spanish. They settled down and lived as farmers on the larger islands, where they grew tobacco on small farms and used the native peoples of the area as slave labour. Because these people had never mixed with Europeans before, they had no resistance to the new diseases which the Spanish brought with them from Europe. By the middle of the sixteenth century so many Indians had died from diseases such as smallpox, and also from ill-treatment, that the Spanish settlers started to buy slaves from West Africa, who were made to work on their plantations.

OTHER EUROPEANS The Spanish were not the only Europeans to colonize islands in the West Indies. Thomas Warner, an Englishman, sighted the island of St. Kitts in 1622 and by 1625 it had both an English

70

Left. This picture shows a sugar cane factory. The cane was cut, bundled up and taken to a press which was driven by a waterwheel. The press squeezed the juice out of the cane. The juice was then boiled in cauldrons until the water evaporated and left the sugar crystals behind.

Below. In the late sixteenth century, English sailors were still able to trade with some of the native people of the West Indies. A hundred years later, both the Arawaks and the Caribs had almost disappeared.

Right. Christopher Columbus visited Hispaniola in 1492 and claimed it for Spain. The native people tried to resist the Spanish, but they only had bows and arrows and spears against guns. By 1496 the Spanish had colonized Hispaniola and about 100,000 of its native population had died of disease, violence or starvation.

The Manioc Plant

Manioc was an important food crop in the West Indies. It had to be processed before it was eaten, as its roots were poisonous. The outer covering was peeled off and the rest was grated into a pulp. The juice was squeezed out and simmered, leaving a syrup which became the base for a stew. The remaining pulp was made into flour.

and a French settlement. From there the English went on to Nevis, Montserrat and Barbados, while the French went to Guadaloupe, Martinique and St. Lucia. The Dutch claimed Curaçao, Aruba and St. Eustatius, but these were mainly used as trading posts.

THE SLAVE TRADE The Europeans had hoped to find treasure in the West Indies. However, all they found were pearls and a small amount of gold. Then in the middle of the seventeenth century they began to grow sugar cane in the islands. Large sugar plantations replaced the small tobacco farms and the slave trade began in earnest. Ships set out from Europe to West Africa carrying cargoes of beads and blankets. These were exchanged for slaves, who were in turn shipped to the West Indies. There the slaves were exchanged for sugar, which was taken back to be sold in Europe, before the ships went back to Africa for more slaves. The slaves were transported in the most primitive conditions. They were chained to the decks and they were so cramped that they could not stand up. Many died on the voyages to the West Indies.

Opening up the World
TIME CHART

	THE AMERICAS	INDIA, CHINA AND JAPAN	AFRICA	REST OF THE WORLD
AD				
1500	Cabral lands briefly in Brazil and claims it for Portugal		Cabral and his ships call at Mozambique and Malindi	
1517			The Ottomans conquer Egypt	
1520				Magellan sails around South America and into the Pacific Suleiman the Magnificent becomes Ottoman emperor
1522	Hernando Cortes defeats the Aztecs in Mexico			
1526		Babur founds the Mogul Dynasty in India		
1528			Askia Muham, the Songhai emperor, is deposed	
1532	Francisco Pizarro defeats the Incas in Peru			
1533				Ivan IV becomes Tsar of Russia
1535	The lands of the Aztecs, Maya and Toltecs become the Vice-Royalty of New Spain			
1543		Portuguese sailors are the first Europeans to visit Japan		
1562			The English sea-captain, John Hawkins, makes a slaving voyage to Sierra Leone.	
1571				The Spanish capture the Philippines The Ottomans are defeated at the Battle of Lepanto
1581				The Russian settlement of Siberia begins
1591			The Songhai Empire is invaded by the Moroccans	
1593			The Portuguese start to build Fort Jesus at Mombasa	
1600		The British East India Company is set up to trade with India		
1602		The Dutch East India Company is formed to trade in spices and other goods from the Far East		
1603		The start of the Tokugawa shogunate in Japan		
1605>1613				The Time of Troubles in Russia
1607	Jamestown is founded by the Virginia Company			
1608	Samuel Champlain founds Quebec			
1619				The Dutch found the colony of Batavia in Indonesia
1620	The Pilgrim Fathers sail from England to America			
1642				Abel Tasman sails to Tasmania and New Zealand
1644		The Ming Dynasty of China is defeated by the Manchus		Abel Tasman sails along the north coast of Australia

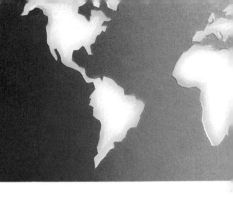

GLOSSARY

alliance An agreement between two countries or governments to co-operate with each other.

astronomer Someone who makes a scientific study of the stars and planets.

bankrupt Someone whose business fails, usually leaving large debts.

barometer An instrument used to measure the air pressure at a particular place on the earth's surface.

Black Death A disease which came to Europe in 1347–48. It was carried by rat fleas and was very infectious. It might have killed up to 50 percent of the population in some areas.

bloomery A simple furnace where iron ore is smelted into metal.

bureaucracy A system in which government officials control the way a country is run.

cantons The different areas which make up the country of Switzerland.

cavalry Soldiers who fight on horseback.

city-states Cities which were large and important enough to have their own systems of government.

colony A group of people who form a settlement in another country, or the settlement that they form.

congregations (Puritan) Groups of people who gathered together to worship according to Puritan ways.

daimyo A feudal lord in Japan.

deposed A ruler removed from power, usually by force.

diocese A number of parishes under the control of a bishop.

dissent To disagree with views that are generally accepted.

Divine Right The idea that a monarch rules a country as God's representative on earth.

dykes Ditches or channels which are dug in order to drain water from low-lying land.

dynasty A period of time during which one family rules a country or empire.

English Prayer Book The prayer book used by people in the Church of England.

excommunicated A person who is cut off by the Church and forbidden to take part in any of its services.

feudal system A way of organizing society, stretching from one powerful, wealthy person (usually a king) to those with no power at all. The king owns all the land, but grants it to others in exchange for military or labor services.

fire ships Old ships which are filled with gunpowder, moved close to enemy ships and then deliberately set on fire.

fulling mill The place where woollen cloth was taken to be washed after it had been taken off the loom.

grammar schools Schools originally founded in the sixteenth century to teach boys Latin.

guild halls The places where groups of craftsmen, called guilds, held their meetings.

gunpowder An explosive powder used to fire guns and cannons.

heathen A word used by Christians or Muslims to describe someone who does not share their beliefs.

heresy An idea or belief that disagrees with the teachings of the Church.

Holy Roman Empire An area of Europe which included much of Germany, Austria and Hungary and which was usually ruled by the Habsburg family.

holy sacraments The ceremonies of the Church, including baptism, communion and burial.

Huguenots French Protestants.

ingots Gold or silver which has been made into solid bars.

Inquisition An official Roman Catholic court which tried people who had been accused of heresy.

junks Chinese cargo ships with square sails.

Kremlin A fortified building in the center of any Russian town, especially the one in Moscow.

lacquerwork Objects, originally from China, that are covered with a varnish made from the sap of the lac tree.

latitude The distance of a place north or south of the Equator.

longitude The distance of a place east or west of a given point.

Lutherans Protestants who follow the teachings of Martin Luther.

malnutrition A weakness caused by not eating enough healthy food.

Middle Ages The period in European history from about the twelfth century to the beginning of the sixteenth century.

missionary work Work done by people, usually Christians, in an attempt to spread their own religion and beliefs.

Mongols People who came from Mongolia. They set up an empire in China in the thirteenth century.

monopoly A right to deal in a certain product which is granted to just one person, or claimed by one country.

musketeers Soldiers who used

guns known as muskets.

open fields A system of farming in which each villager worked a number of strips of land in the same field. They were called open fields because they had no hedges or walls.

Orthodox Christian Someone who follows the beliefs of the part of the Christian Church which broke away from Rome in 1054.

packhorses Horses that were used to carry packs of goods for sale, at a time when the roads were too rough for wheeled vehicles.

parish An area with its own church and priest or vicar.

penance A punishment for a religious sin.

persecution Treating people badly because of their religious or political beliefs.

philosophy Seeking for wisdom and knowledge, especially about people, their ideas and beliefs.

pike-men Soldiers who fought with weapons called pikes, rather than with guns.

pilgrims People who went on journeys to visit important religious sites.

porcelain Very fine pottery which has a hard glaze, or sheen.

Protestants Christians who broke away from the Roman Catholic Church during the Reformation.

quadrant An instrument shaped like a quarter of a circle and used for measuring angles.

Renaissance The period in European history when people rediscovered the work and learning of the Ancient Greeks and Romans, and expanded on them.

salvation The religious belief that one can please God through prayer and good deeds.

samurai A Japanese warrior, usually in the private army of a feudal lord.

sea-astrolabe An instrument used to measure the height of stars above the horizon from a ship that is at sea.

serfdom A system in which peasants had to work in one particular place for one particular landowner and had no right to move or to own property.

sultan The ruler of the Ottoman Empire.

Tartars Another name for the Mongols who invaded Russia.

taxation The way in which the government of a country raises money from its people.

tenter-frame A large, wooden frame on which wet cloth was stretched into shape after it had been to the fulling mill.

theology The study of religion.

treason To plot or act against the ruler or government of a country.

tribute An amount paid in goods or money by a conquered people to their conqueror.

vestments Special robes worn by priests during a church service.

viceroy Someone who rules in a colony on behalf of a monarch of another country.

wall paintings Pictures painted on the walls of churches to tell stories from the Bible.

INDEX

Further Reading

GENERAL

The Times Atlas of World Exploration by Times Books Staff (HarperCollins, 1991)

Fourteen Ninety-Two: the Year of the New World by Piero Ventura (Putnam, 1992)

Renaissance by Francene Sabin (Troll, 1985)

The Renaissance and the New World by Giovanni Caselli (Bedrick, Peter, 1986)

EUROPE

Early Modern Europe: 1500–1789 by H. G. Koenigsberger (Longman, 1987)

The Tudor Age by Jasper Ridley (Overlook, 1990)

Mary Tudor: a Life by David Loades (Blackwell, 1992)

Henry VIII: the Politics of Tyranny by Jasper Ridley (Fromm, 1986)

Elizabeth I: the Shrewdness of Virtue by Jasper Ridley (Fromm, 1989)

The Spanish Armada by Colin Martin (Norton, 1988)

Voyage of the Armada by David Howarth (Viking Penguin, 1982)

Cromwell: the Lord Protector by Antonia Fraser (Fine, 1986)

Mary, Queen of Scots by Antonia Fraser (Dell, 1984)

Ivan the Terrible by Henri Troyat (Berkley, 1986)

A Weekend With Rembrandt by Pascal Bonafoux (Rizzoli, 1992)

The Thirty Years' War ed. by Geoffrey Parker, (Routledge, 1988)

Jamestown: the Beginning (Little, Brown, 1974)

THE REST OF THE WORLD

A History of the Pacific Islands by Ian Campbell (U. of California, 1990)

Atlas of African History by Colin McEvedy (Viking Penguin, 1980)

Africa in History by Basil Davidson (Macmillan, 1992)

Lost Cities of Africa by Basil Davidson (Little, Brown, 1988)

The Ancient Kingdoms of Mexico by Nigel Davies (Viking Penguin, 1984)

Conquistadors by Jean Descola (Kelley, 1970)

Picture Acknowledgements

The author and publishers would like to acknowledge, with thanks,
the following photographic sources:
p. 10 Bridgeman Art Library; p. 11 (upper) Giraudon; p. 11 (centre) AKG; p. 11 (lower) AKG;
p. 12 Robert Harding Picture Library; p. 13 Bulloz; p. 14 Mansell Collection; p. 15 AKG; p. 17
Mary Evans Picture Library; p. 18 (left) Bridgeman Art Library; p. 18 (centre) AKG; p. 18
(right) Michael Holford; p. 20 Tiroler Landesmuseum Ferdinandeum; p. 21 (upper) AKG; p. 21
(lower) Mansell Collection; p. 22 (upper) Mary Evans Picture Library; p. 22 (lower) Mansell
Collection; p. 23 Ancient Art & Architecture Collection; p. 24 Crown Copyright; The Royal
Armouries; p. 25 Robert Harding Picture Library; p. 26 Ancient Art & Architecture Collection;
p. 27 Giraudon; p. 28 Robert Harding Picture Library; p. 29 Bridgeman Art Library; p. 31
Robert Harding Picture Library; p. 32 Giraudon; p. 33 Mary Evans Picture Library; p. 34
Musees Royaux de Beaux-Arts de Belgique; p. 35 (left) Giraudon; p. 35 (right) AKG; p. 36
(upper) Robert Harding Picture Library; p. 36 (lower left) Mansell Collection, p. 36 (lower
centre) Bulloz; p. 36 (lower right) AKG; p. 37 Mansell Collection; p. 38 Guttenberg Museum;
p. 43 (left) Mansell Collection, p. 43 (right) AKG; p. 45 Michael Holford; p. 46 Werner Forman
Archive, p. 47 (left) National Portrait Gallery, p. 47 (right) Sheepvaartmuseum; p. 49 (upper &
lower) Mansell Collection; p. 50 Hulton-Deutsch Collection; p. 51 Mansell Collection; p. 52 Sonia
Halliday Photographs; p. 53 Michael Holford; p. 55 (left) Osterreichische Nationalbibliotek, p. 55
(right) National Museum, Copenhagen; p. 56 Roger Hammond, p. 57 (upper) Robert Harding
Picture Library; p. 57 (lower left & right) Michael Holford; p. 58 Bridgeman Art Library; p. 62
Werner Forman Archive; p. 63 (upper left) Hulton-Deutsch Collection, p. 63 (upper right) Robert
Harding Picture Library; p. 63 (lower left, centre & right) Trustees of the British Museum; p. 64
(upper) Trustees of the British Museum, p. 64 (centre) Hulton-Deutsch Collection, p. 64 (lower
left) Werner Forman Archive, p. 64 (lower right) Trustees of the British Library; p. 66 AKG;
p. 67 (upper & lower left) South American Pictures, p. 67 (upper right) Michael Holford, p. 67
(lower right) Courtesy of the Hispanic Society of America; p. 69 Mansell Collection; p.70
Trustees of the British Museum; p. 71 Hulton-Deutsch Collection. Wherever possible the
copyright holder has been notified but we apologize if any material appears in error.